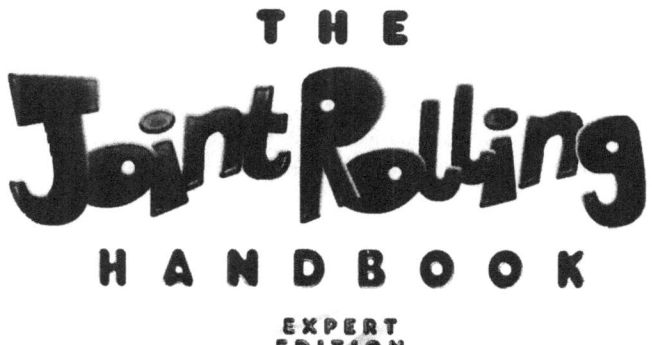

This book contains information about illegal substances, specifically the plant *Cannabis sativa* and its derivative products. Quick Trading Company and Echo Point Books & Media would like to emphasize that *Cannabis* is a controlled substance in the United States and throughout much of the world. As such, the use and cultivation of *Cannabis* can carry heavy penalties that may threaten an individual's liberty and livelihood.

The aim of the publishers is to educate and entertain. Whatever the publishers' view of the validity of current legislation, we do not in any way condone the use of prohibited substances.

Reprinted by arrangement with Quick Trading Company, Piedmont, CA

Published by Echo Point Books & Media
Brattleboro, Vermont
www.EchoPointBooks.com

All rights reserved.
Neither this work nor any portions thereof may be reproduced, stored in a retrieval system, or transmitted in any capacity without written permission from the publisher.

Copyright © 1997, 2022 by Richard Kemplay

Joint Rolling Handbook: Expert Editon
ISBN: 978-1-64837-161-5 (casebound)
        978-1-64837-162-2 (paperback)

Project Manager: Andrew McBeth
Editor: Lize McBeth
Coloration: Larry Utley
Additional Typesetting: Nancy Koerner
Cover design by Kaitlyn Whitaker

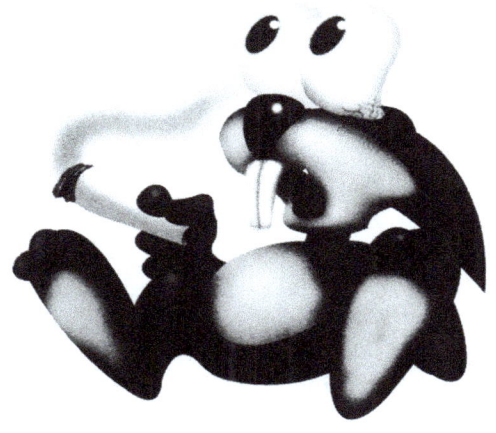

TABLE OF CONTENTS

CONTENTS

17
Secret Agent

6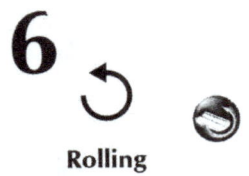
Rolling

20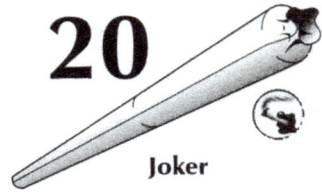
Joker

8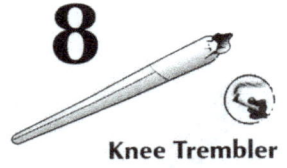
Knee Trembler

23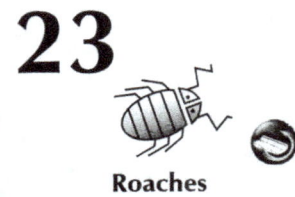
Roaches

10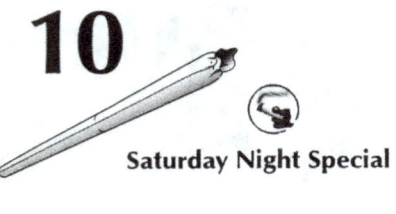
Saturday Night Special

24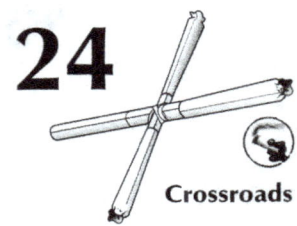
Crossroads

12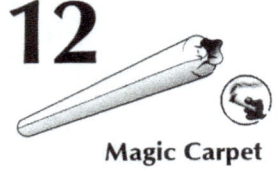
Magic Carpet

27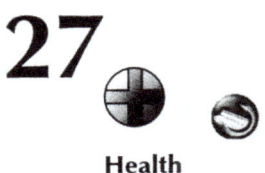
Health

14
The Mix

CONTENTS

29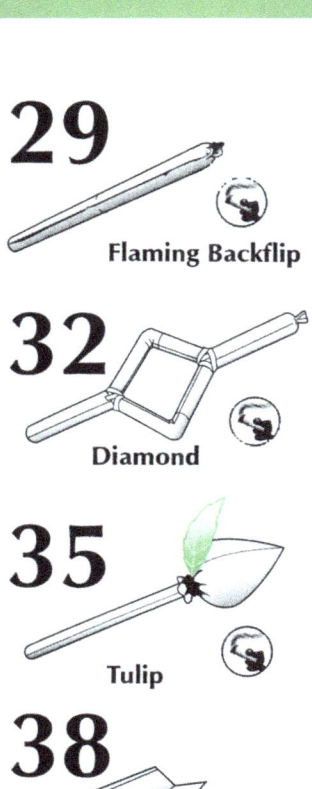
Flaming Backflip

32
Diamond

35
Tulip

38
Paper

40
Nose Cone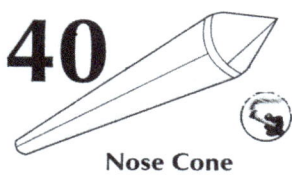

43
Windmill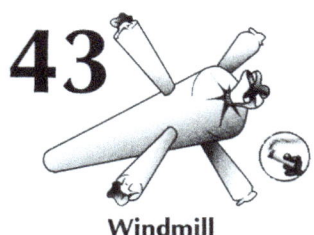

46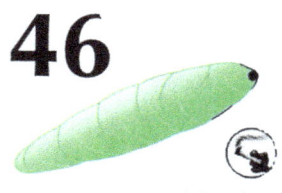
Cannabis Cigar

50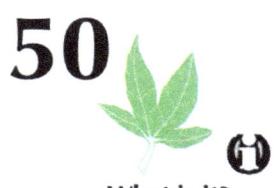
What is it?

52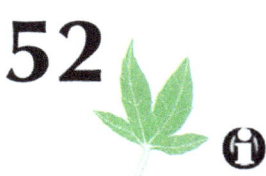
Being Stoned

54
Post-Stoned

58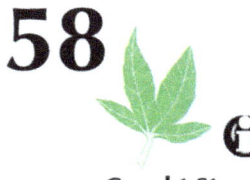
Caught Stoned

ROLLING

MOST PEOPLE READING THIS HANDBOOK WILL BE WELL PRACTICED IN THE ART OF ROLLING A DECENT, SMOKABLE JOINT. HOWEVER, FOR THOSE WITH MORE THUMBS THAN FINGERS AND A ZERO-RATING ON THE KUDOS SCALE, HERE ARE A FEW BASIC TIPS . . .

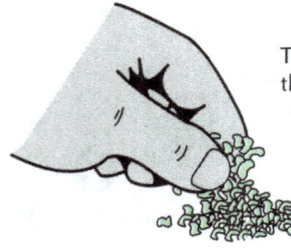

The mix is perhaps the most important part of the joint (*see page 14*). Make sure the consistency is even and break up or remove any lumps or "woody" bits.

The shape of the finished joint is determined by how you distribute the mix over the papers. Many of the joints in the book are cone-shaped. Cones tend to smoke more smoothly than straight joints but are slightly harder to roll.

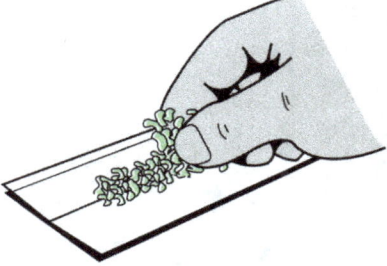

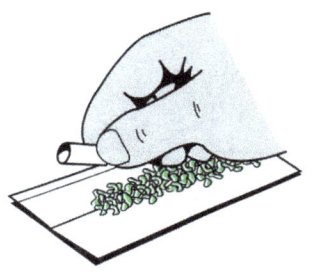

Putting the roach in BEFORE rolling is highly recommended and saves time and hassle (see page 23). You're also more likely to get a perfect fit.

Now for the "tricky" bit. Pick everything up and start in the middle, rolling outward. Let your thumbs do most of the work and give support and pressure with your forefingers. You should start to feel the mix firming inside the paper.

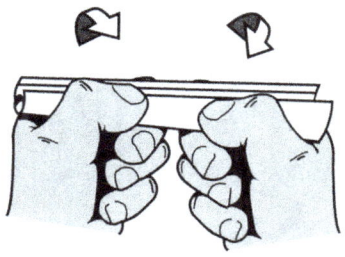

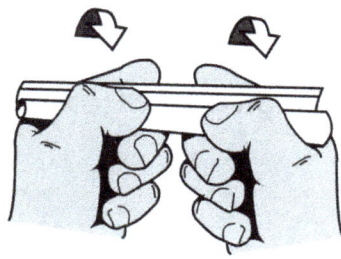

When you have an even consistency, tuck down the facing paper edge with the tips of your thumbs, wrap the excess paper around the joint, wet the glue and seal that baby!

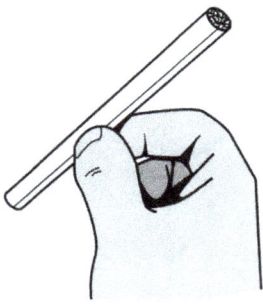

The best joints are firm but not so tight you have to bust a lung drawing smoke. Loose joints taste rough, burn too fast and have a nasty habit of setting fire to clothing and furniture.

Knee Trembler

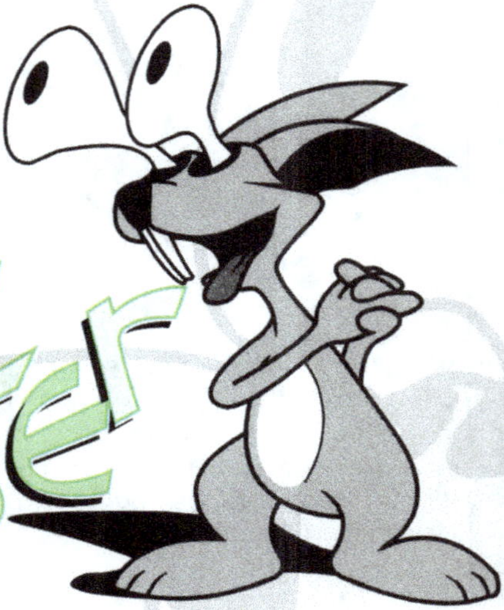

PERFECT FOR ROLLING IN AWKWARD SITUATIONS, THE TREMBLER IS SPEEDY, SIMPLE, USES ONLY TWO PAPERS AND COMES HIGHLY RECOMMENDED. A CLASSIC QUICKIE.

1

Stick two papers together at a 45° angle as shown.

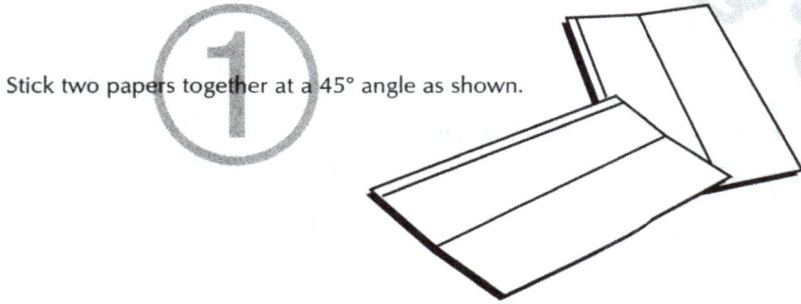

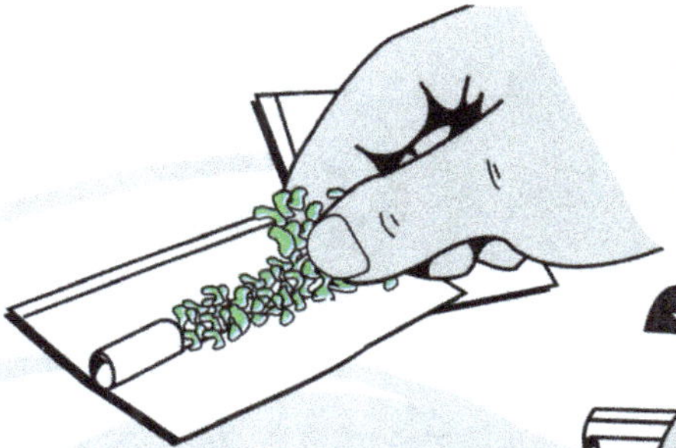

Add the mix and the roach. The layout of the papers makes the Trembler perfect for a cone shaped creation.

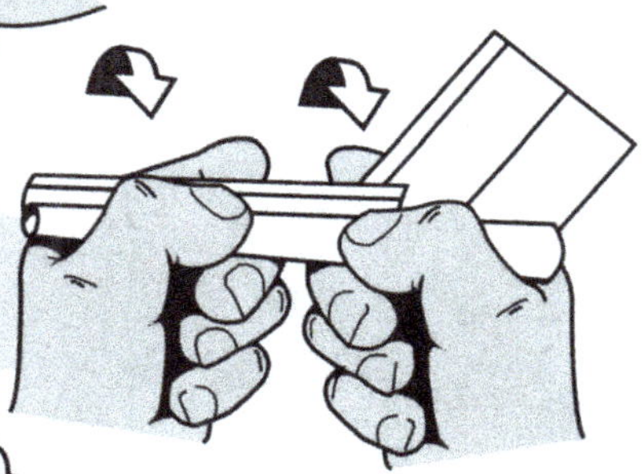

When rolling the joint, stick down the first paper . . .

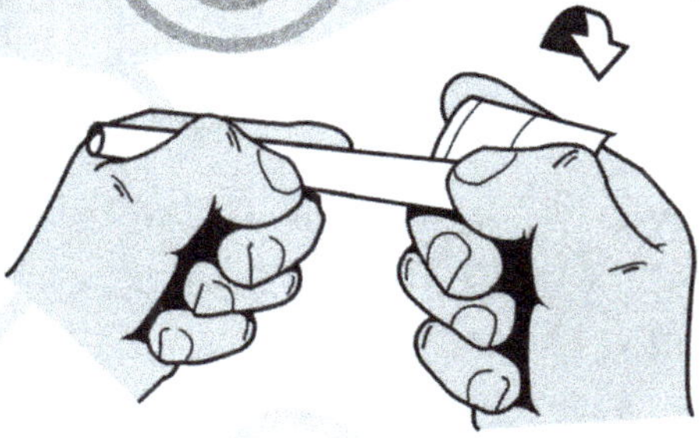

. . . before wetting the second and then wrapping it around to seal the smoking end of the joint. Voilà!

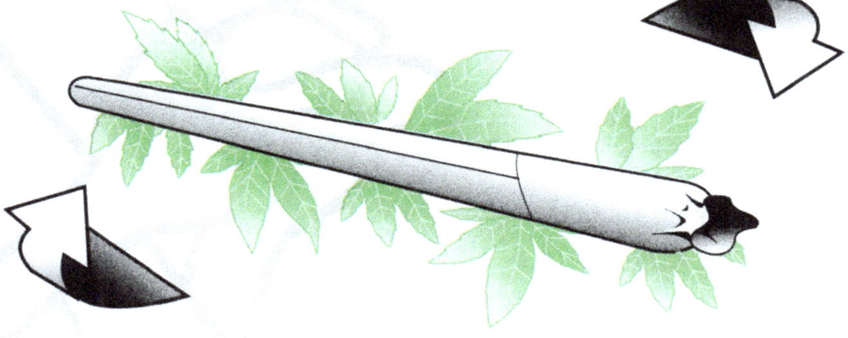

Saturday Night Special

An undisputed classic, well known to most smokers, the Special is easy to roll and tolerates clumsy fingers. Everyone has a favorite way of rolling the Special—this is just one of them.

Stick two papers together with the gum strips forming a straight line. They should overlap by about a fifth of their length.

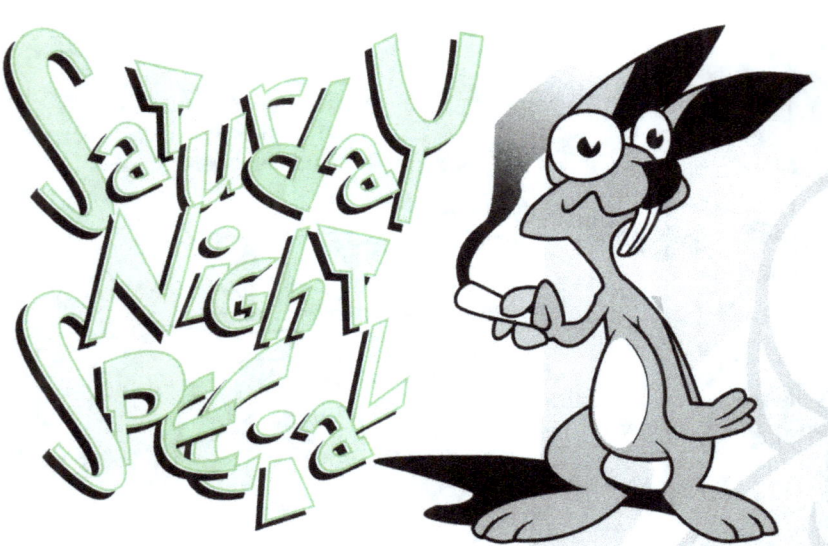

①

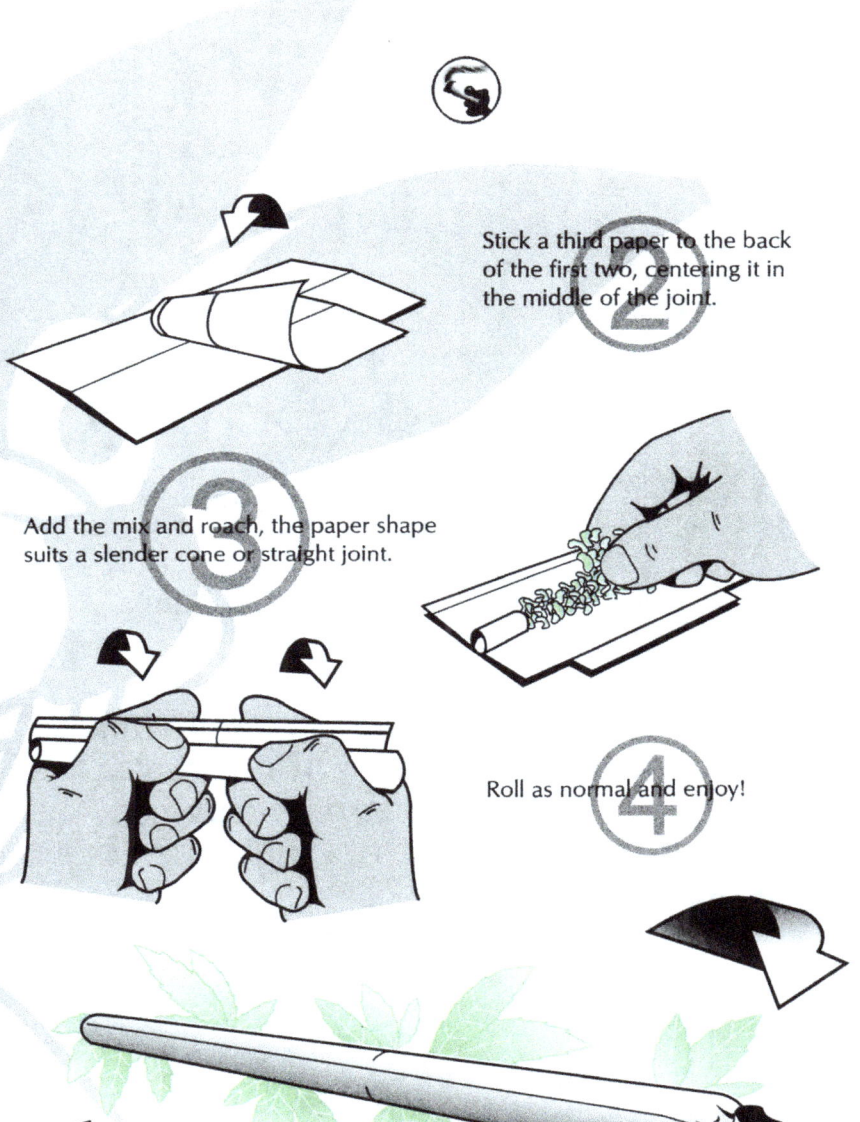

Stick a third paper to the back of the first two, centering it in the middle of the joint.

Add the mix and roach, the paper shape suits a slender cone or straight joint.

Roll as normal and enjoy!

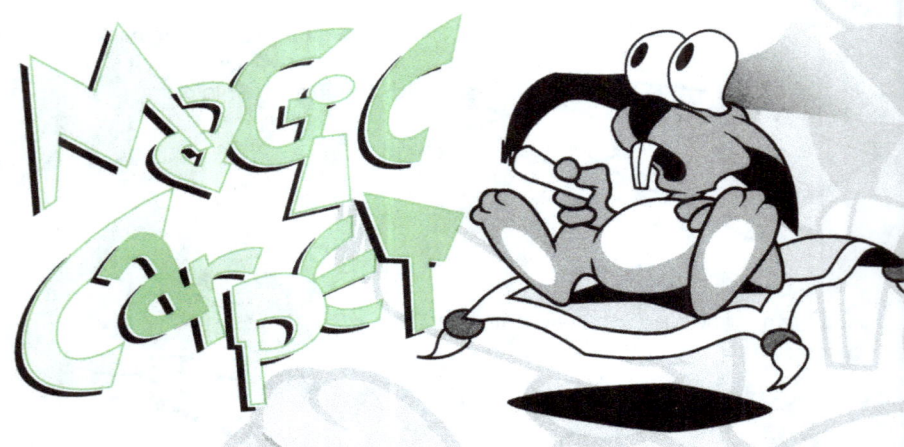

Magic Carpet

FLY INTO FANTASY ON THE AXMINSTER OF YOUR DREAMS! POPULAR IN NORTH AFRICA, WHERE A CIGARETTE SEGMENT IS SUBSTITUTED FOR THE ROACH, THE CARPET IS IDEAL FOR THOSE WHO LIKE THEM SHORT AND FAT.

Stick two papers together to form a square with a gummed strip along one side.

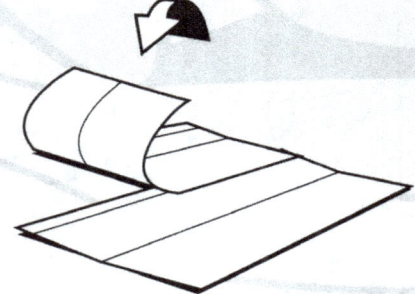

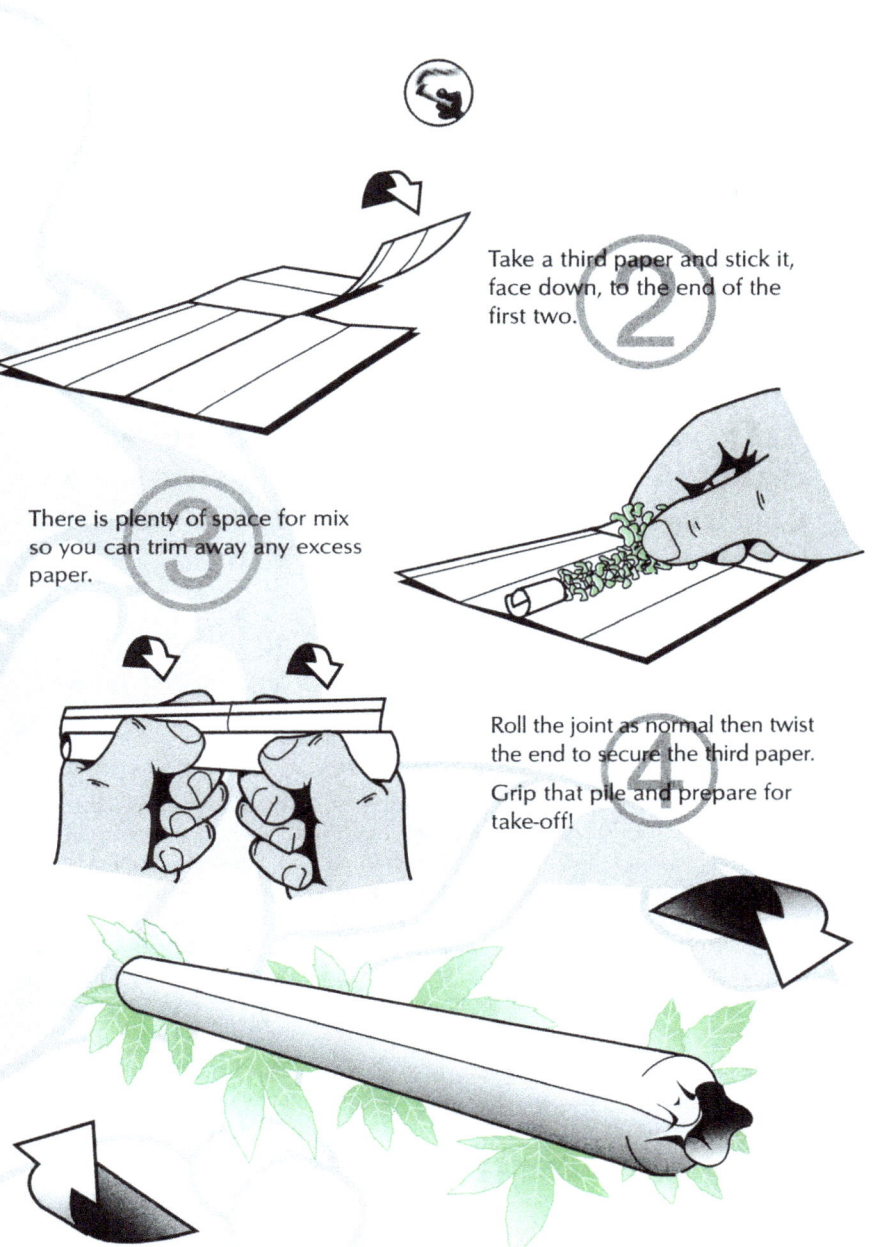

Take a third paper and stick it, face down, to the end of the first two.

There is plenty of space for mix so you can trim away any excess paper.

Roll the joint as normal then twist the end to secure the third paper.

Grip that pile and prepare for take-off!

THE MIX

Getting the mix right is half the art of joint-rolling. There's plenty of scope for choice but quantity is never a substitute for quality—don't waste your lungs on inferior ingredients.

The female's flower-tops are by far the most potent part of the cannabis plant. Thanks to cannabis farmers all around the world there are thousands of strains and varieties—the quality, strength and nature of which can differ enormously.

Imported bud is often force-dried and compressed for storage/transit purposes, this can simply be broken up and crumbled into the mix. Better quality bud which has been properly cured and stored is more delicate. The flower heads should be handled with care to protect the delicate THC glands. Use sharp scissors to break up the bud and store the remainder in a cool, dark place. Discard any seeds or stems as they contain little THC and are harsh to smoke. Fresh bud may develop mold if stored incorrectly and (painful as it may be) this should be thrown away as it can damage the lungs and cause infection.

The Skunk or Nederweit varieties which are genetically bred for extreme potency should be used sparingly until the user is familiar with, and can predict, their effects.

WARNING: THIS SUBSTANCE IS ILLEGAL IN THE UNITED STATES.

Cannabis leaf is a common ingredient in commercial weed. If you can stand the slightly acrid taste, some leaf—especially that from the top of a flowering female plant—can be surprisingly potent. Only use well-cured leaves and remove any stems before crumbling them into the mix. The larger "sun" leaves from around the lower part of the plant are too harsh for use in joint-rolling and are best left for the water pipe.

WARNING: THIS SUBSTANCE IS ILLEGAL IN THE UNITED STATES.

Hashish comes in many different forms from hard and rocky Lebanese to soft and oily Nepalese. As with all cannabis there is a huge variation in quality. The very best hashish is made by rubbing the sticky resin from flowering-tops. Most however, contains processed plant material and binding agents and the worst is adulterated with chemicals. Hash is normally heated with a flame, crumbled into a powder and then mixed with tobacco or herbal smoking material. Good hashish should burn and crumble with ease. Alternatively, very soft hash can be rolled into thin "sausages" and placed along the length of the joint.

NEVER over-fill joints with hash, or use large chunks—it will burn badly and much will be wasted. A brief spell in the microwave will give you a perfect hashish and herbal blend.

WARNING: THIS SUBSTANCE IS ILLEGAL IN THE UNITED STATES.

Genuine resin oil is very hard to come by but, if you can get it, the Real McCoy is incredibly potent. It comes in the form of a black, brown or transparent oily fluid which is smeared across the rolling papers or blended into the mix. Consumers in the Netherlands should be aware that the country's relaxed drug policy does not extend to this substance.

WARNING: THIS SUBSTANCE IS ILLEGAL IN THE UNITED STATES.

Legal highs have come a long way in the last few years. Although claims of effects comparable to the "real thing" are usually false there are many genuinely psychoactive and therapeutic herbs which can be used as ingredients in a smoking mix. Legal smoking mixtures can be a good alternative to tobacco and are the only option for smokers seeking a buzz under cannabis prohibition. There is some evidence that certain herbs can amplify the effects of more psychoactive substances. Always follow the instructions supplied.

While the ingredients are a matter of choice, taste and legal availability, a good mix is always a consistent one. Uneven mixes burn erratically, often resulting in collapsed joints and wasted bud. Making your mix before adding it to the joint is highly recommended. Experienced smokers sometimes make the mix in the palm of their hand and then flip this onto the papers, others use a mixing bowl.

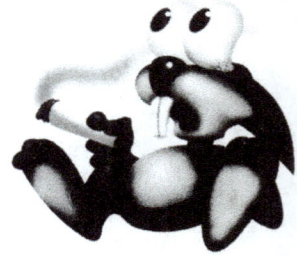

Secret Agent

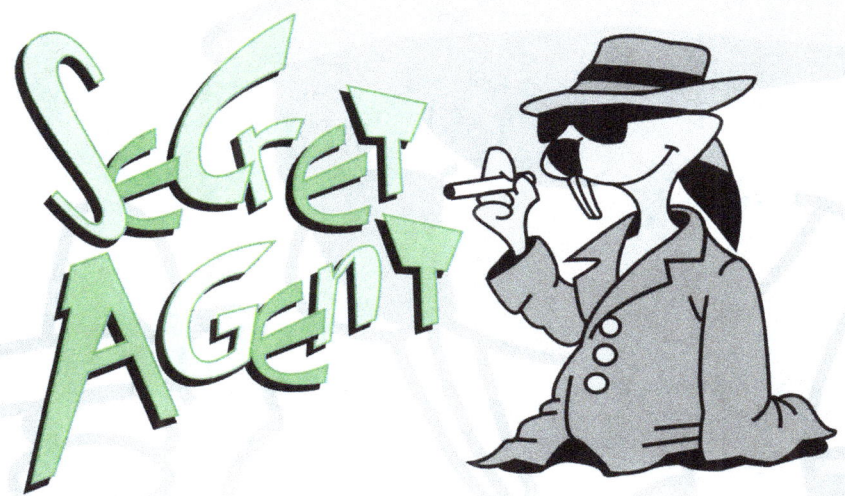

Joint smoking often demands a little discretion. If you're in the need for a clandestine toke, roll yourself a Secret Agent and remember to stay downwind.

Stick two papers together to make a square with a gummed strip along one side.

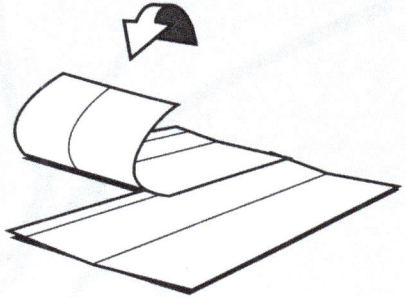

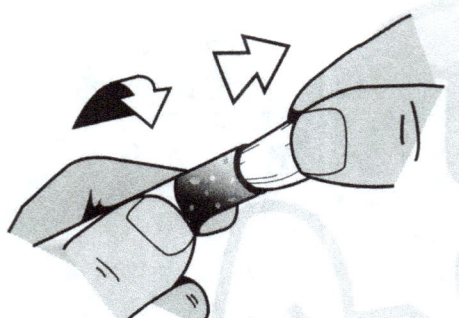

Take a cigarette and remove the filter by squeezing at its base and rotating between finger and thumb. Eventually enough of the filter will show for you to pull it out.

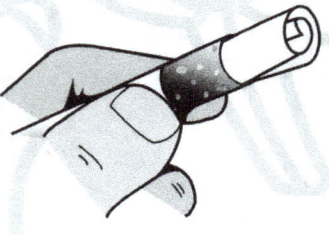

Replace the filter with a roach of the same size and shape.

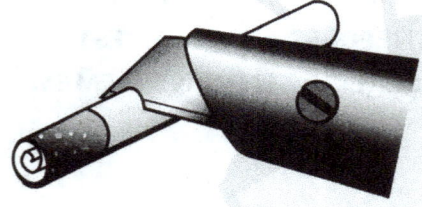

Cut the cigarette in two, as cleanly as possible, about $3/8$ inch from the roach.

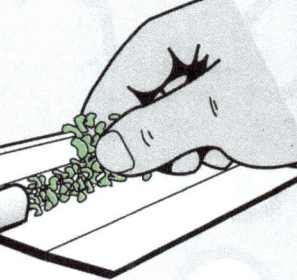

Make up enough mix to replace the tobacco that was cut away and add this to the papers. Form it into the shape of a cigarette.

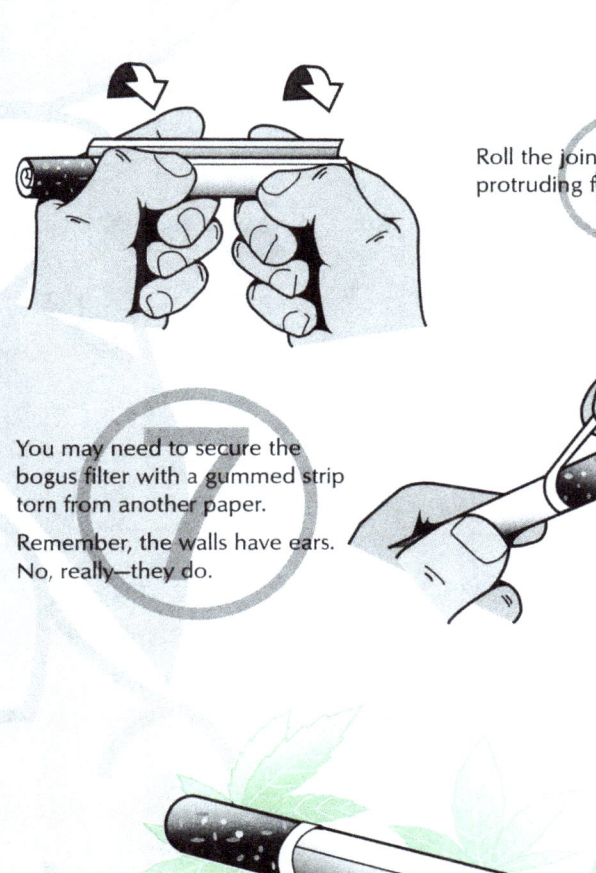

Roll the joint with the "filter" protruding from the end.

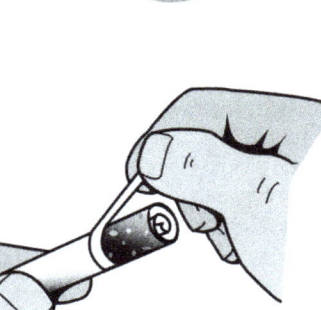

You may need to secure the bogus filter with a gummed strip torn from another paper.

Remember, the walls have ears. No, really—they do.

JOKER

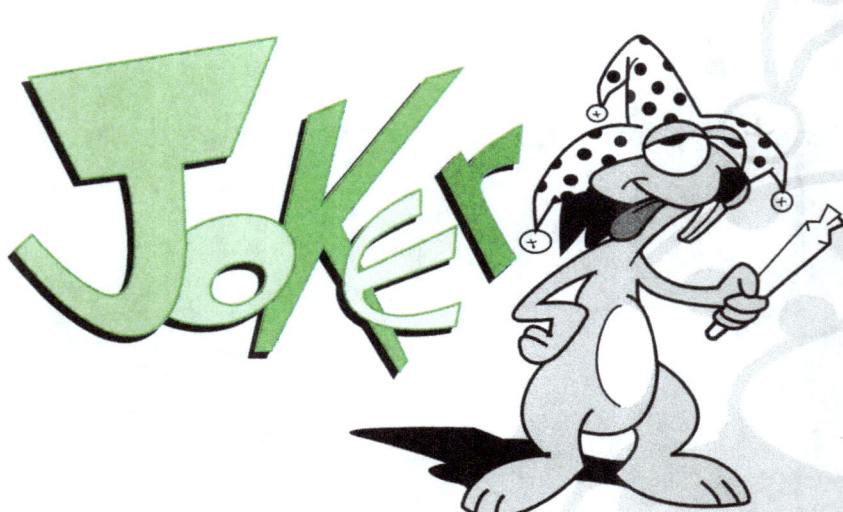

A NUMBER THAT SEEMS TO LAST FOREVER, THE JOKER IS A BIG, FAT, JUICY CONE GUARANTEED TO SPREAD A GRIN FROM EAR-TO-EAR WITHOUT STRAINING THE FINGER MUSCLES.

1. Stick two papers together with the gummed strips forming a straight line.

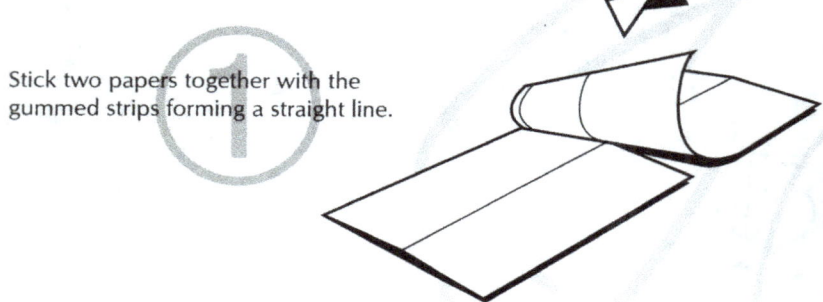

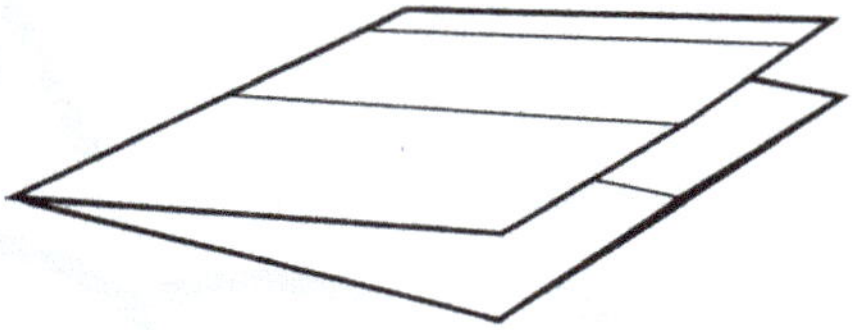

Take a third paper and fold it in half, leaving the gummed strip on the outside.

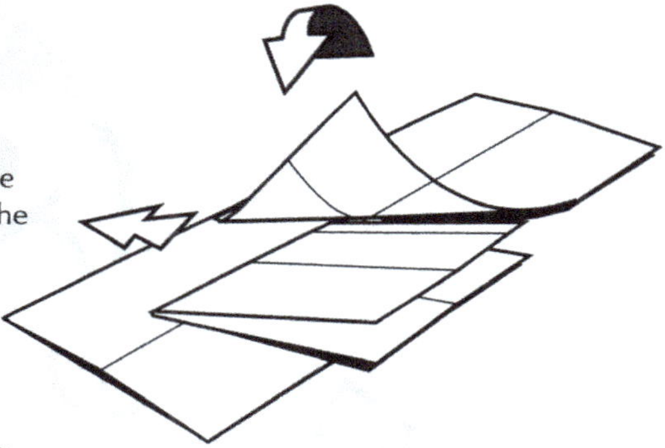

Wet the glue and sandwich the folded paper firmly between the other two as shown.

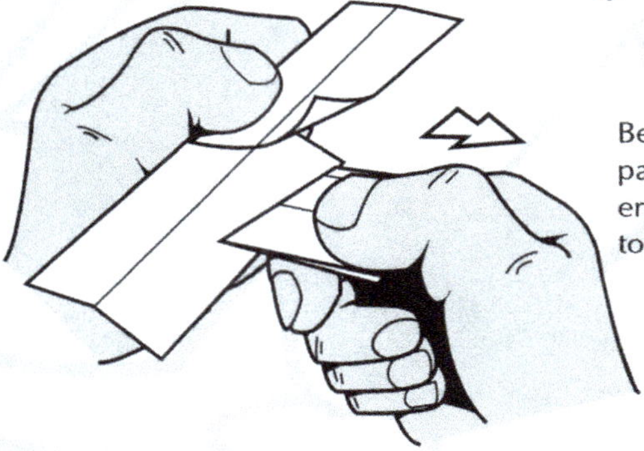

Before the glue dries pull the paper out. It should have left enough glue to stick the others together.

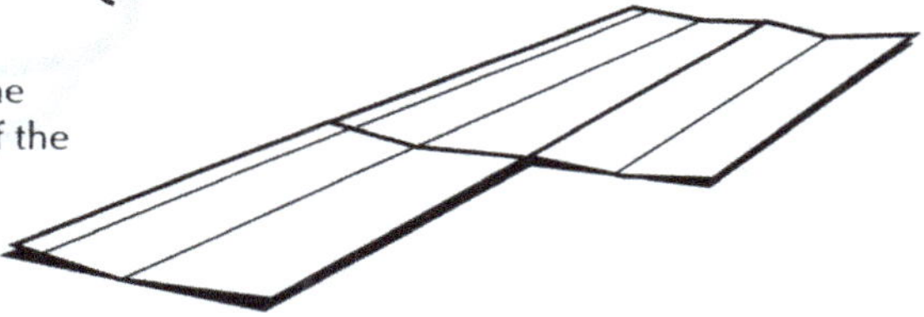

Stick a fourth paper to the lower, right-hand edge of the joint as shown.

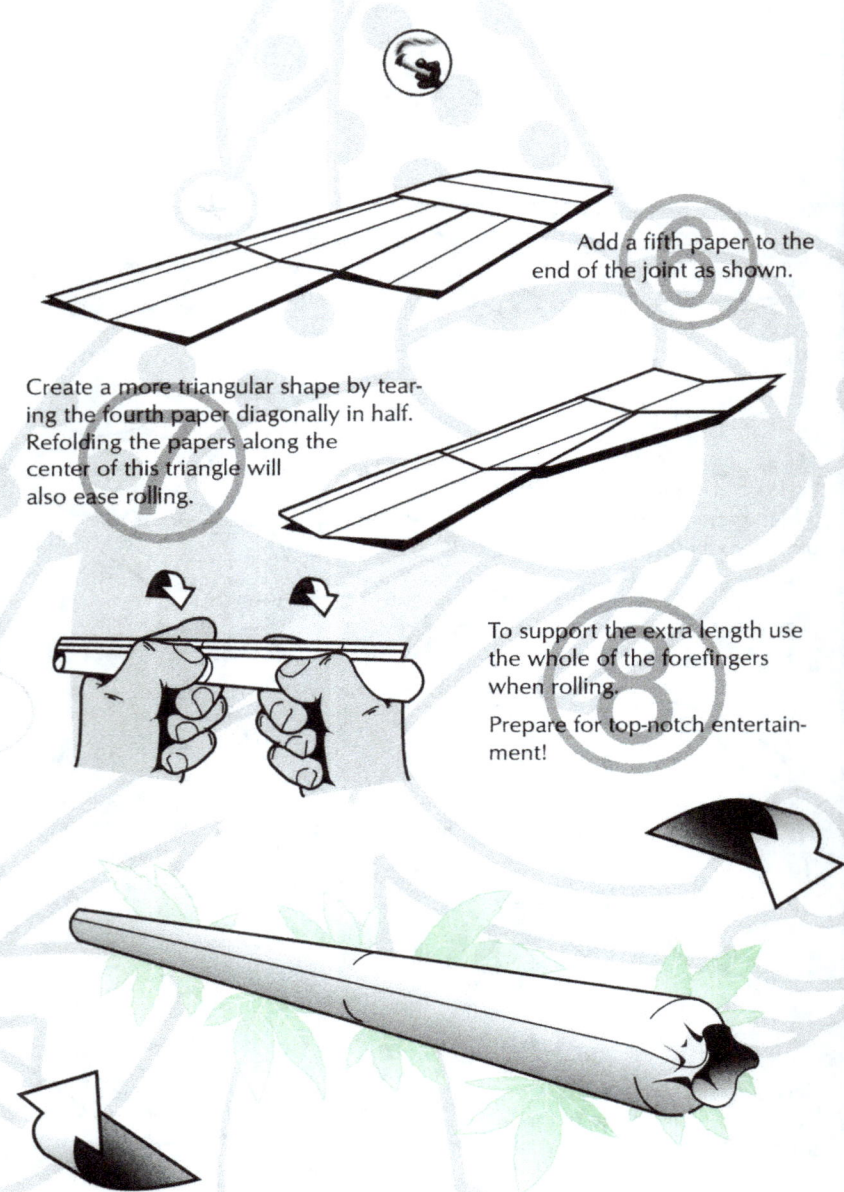

Add a fifth paper to the end of the joint as shown.

Create a more triangular shape by tearing the fourth paper diagonally in half. Refolding the papers along the center of this triangle will also ease rolling.

To support the extra length use the whole of the forefingers when rolling.

Prepare for top-notch entertainment!

THE ROACH

Roaches don't filter the smoke but they do allow it to flow. A good roach also stops the joint from dissolving in your mouth or burning your lips when you chase that last elusive toke. Here's how to make a good one.

The shape and size of roach is down to personal taste. Wide roaches can make the smoke rough whereas tight ones tend to clog, so somewhere in the middle is probably best.

Plain, unprinted card stock is healthier, as some printing inks can emit poisonous fumes when burnt. An excellent roach can be made from a $7/8$ inch by $2 3/4$ inch strip of thin card. Tightly roll the card at a slight angle so that the end of the roach is conical. Roll your joint with the roach already inside (conical end facing outward) and let the card spring out a little to allow the smoke to flow.

Some smokers prefer to insert the roach after making the joint, others find that putting the roach in before rolling makes for a neater fit and a speedier roll. Go with what suits you.

Check out the joint pages for some roaches that do more than just act as mouthpieces.

Crossroads

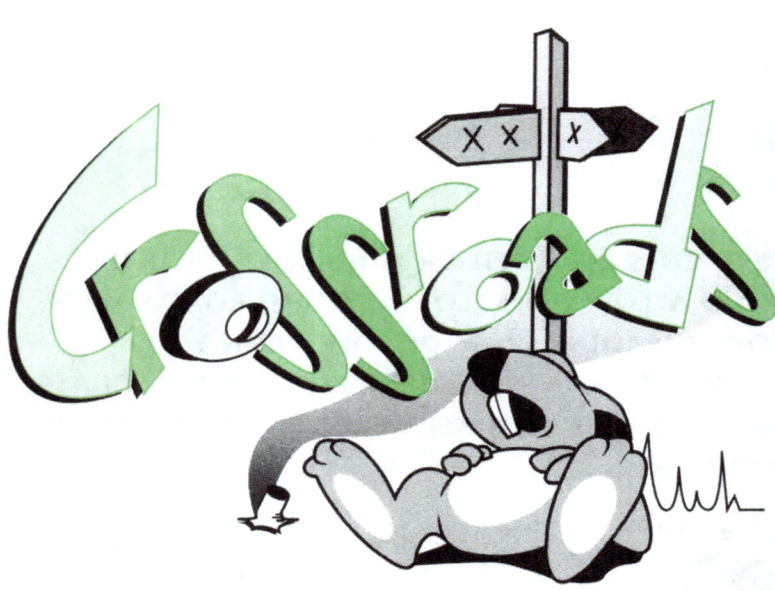

THREE-WAY HEAVEN FOR GOURMANDS! OKAY, OKAY, SO IT'S COMPLICATED, BUT YOU CAN USE IT AGAIN AND AGAIN. BEST OF ALL, IT'LL HOLD THREE OF YOUR FAVORITES.

Make a roach the length and diameter of a thick pencil and seal it with papers or tape.

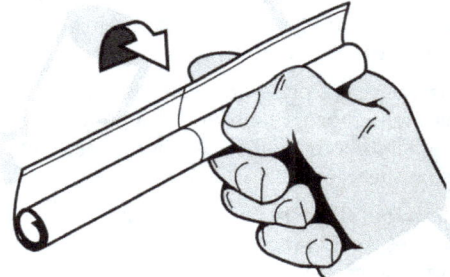

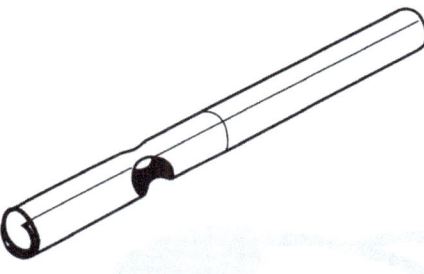

Cut two large, circular holes either side of the first roach, about 1⅛ inch from its end.

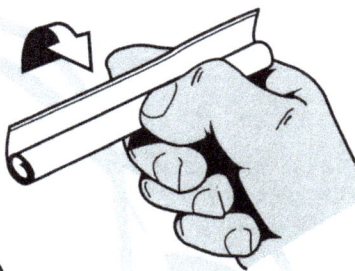

Make a second roach, half the length and slightly narrower than the first.

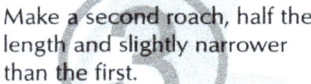

Cut the biggest possible hole you can make through the center of the second roach.

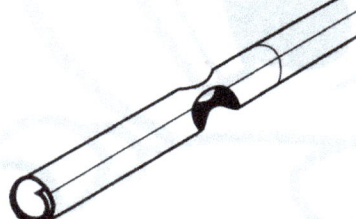

Join the two roaches by inserting the second tube through the hole you made in the first. Rotate the smaller tube until the central smoke hole is in line with the larger tube. If you can see through all the tubes then you've done it.

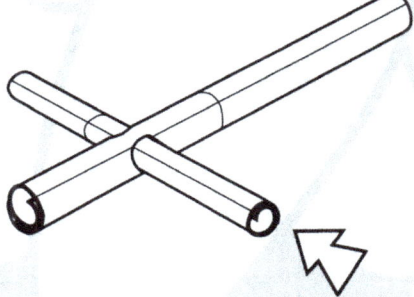

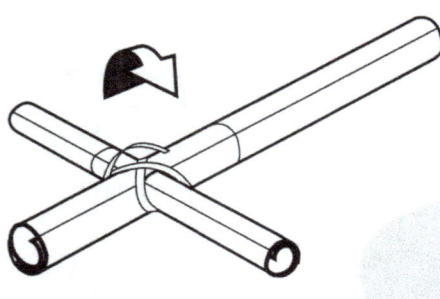

Carefully seal the joins with tape or gummed strips. Keep bandaging until you are sure everything is completely airtight.

To use the roach simply add the joints of your choice to the protruding roaches. Any joints will work, although it does help if they burn at the same rate. Bingo!

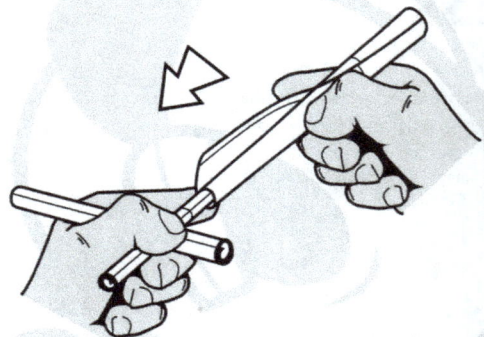

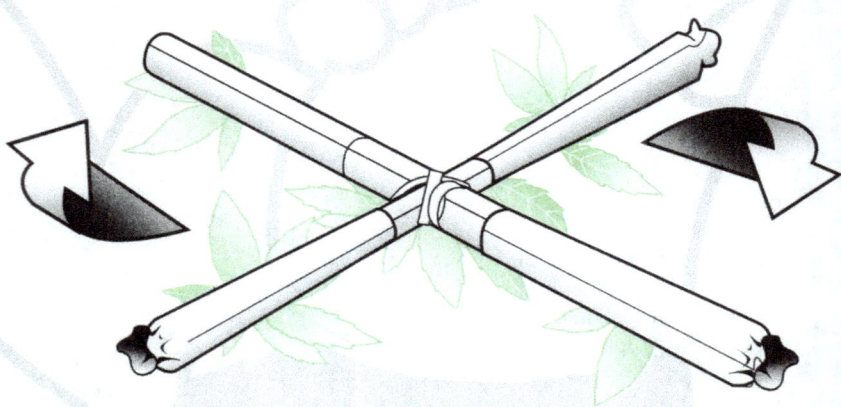

HEALTH

CANNABIS HAS BEEN SHOWN TO BE A NON-ADDICTIVE AND RELATIVELY HARMLESS SUBSTANCE. HOWEVER, INHALING ANY TYPE OF SMOKE COULD NEVER BE DESCRIBED AS ENTIRELY SAFE. DESPITE THIS, STEPS CAN BE TAKEN TO LIMIT DAMAGE AND PROTECT HEALTH.

Cannabis contains more tar than tobacco and hits the throat and lungs at a higher temperature; however, there is little evidence that any significant damage is caused by the amounts normally smoked.

Good quality, pure, herbal cannabis is generally easiest on the lungs. Potency also plays a part—the stronger the weed the less you need to smoke, in theory at any rate. Avoid smoking seeds and low-grade hash containing additives.

Paper produces tar when burnt, and it doesn't get you high. Basically, the less you use the better. The very light-weight varieties are ideal. Always tear off any excess and try rolling in reverse (see page 29) to use the absolute minimum. From all the papers available, wheat straw and rice papers are deemed the healthiest—although we're not exactly sure why.

The best advice for protecting health is to smoke as little as possible. In practice that might mean smoking one strong joint rather than three mediocre ones. Use as little paper and tobacco as possible and don't waste your lungs on poor-quality ingredients.

To minimize the health risks keep the following advice in mind: don't inhale too deeply; don't hold smoke for too long; make sure the room is properly ventilated; avoid "novelty" smoking (shotguns, blow-backs, etc.); and avoid smoking down to the roach.

Standard cigarette filters don't work too well in joints, however the reusable plastic type are worth a try as they can considerably reduce your tar intake. Smoking a joint through a water pipe removes virtually all the carcinogens present in tobacco and cannabis smoke. Pipes specifically designed for this purpose are available from some specialty shops or you can adapt your own. Finally, if you have any sort of respiratory disease, avoid smoking entirely—try some hash cakes or pot cookies instead (where legal, of course)!

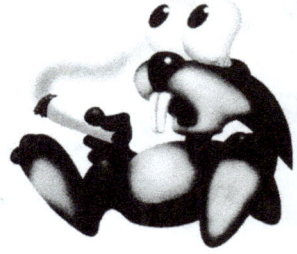

Flaming Backflip

GUARANTEED TO IMPRESS WITH ITS PYROTECHNICS, THE BACKFLIP MAKES USE OF THE MINIMUM OF PAPER AND IS EASY-GOING ON THE LUNGS. PREPARE FOR INSTANT KUDOS OR INSTANT EMBARRASSMENT — THIS IS A TRICKY ONE.

Stick two papers together with the gummed strips forming a straight line.

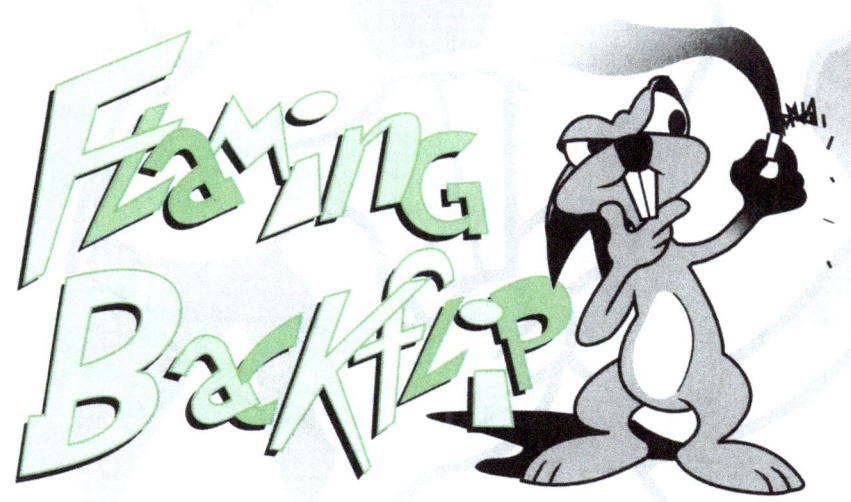

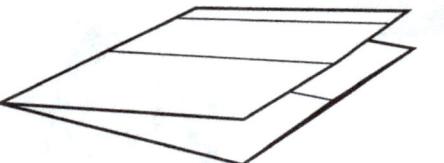

Take a third paper and fold it in half, leaving the gummed strip on the outside.

Wet the gum and sandwich the folded paper firmly between the other two skins, as shown.

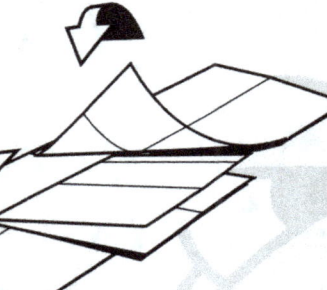

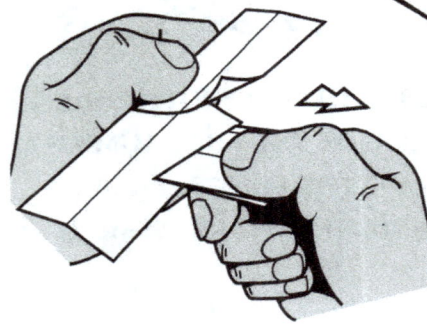

Before the gum dries carefully pull out the third paper. It should leave enough gum behind to stick the other two papers together.

Add the mix to the REVERSE of the papers, keeping the gummed strip facing DOWN and AWAY from you.

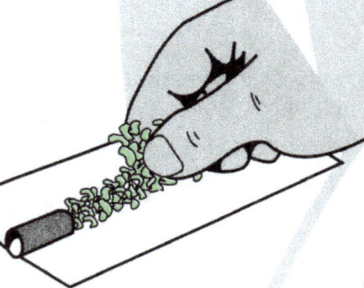

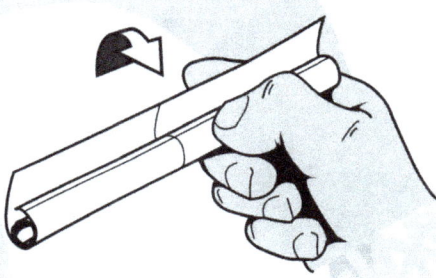

Roll the joint in reverse with the glue on the OUTSIDE. Seal the joint, leaving the excess paper on the outside. N.B. this takes some practice.

Now for the finale. As soon as you have sealed the joint, light the excess paper at the roach. Hold the joint upright and let the flame burn away the unwanted paper as it travels up the joint. If you are lucky the joint should self-ignite.

Bud-a-bing! Kudos is yours!

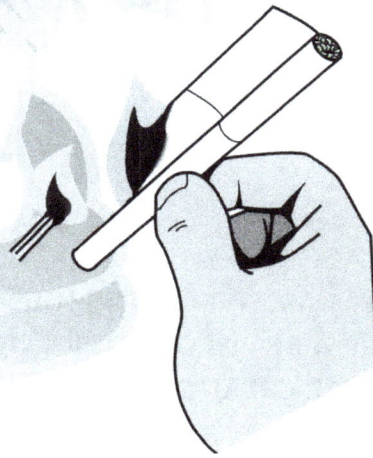

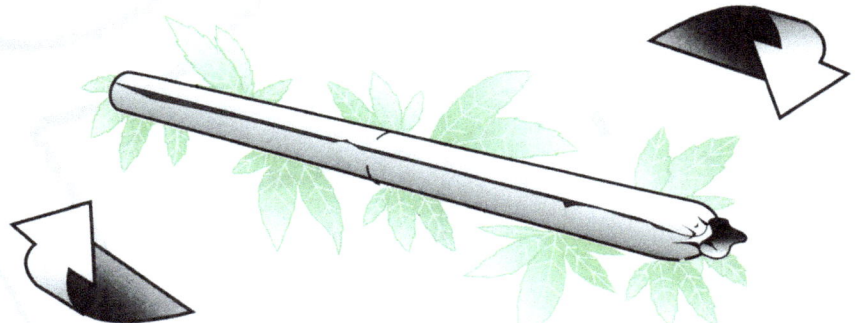

Diamond

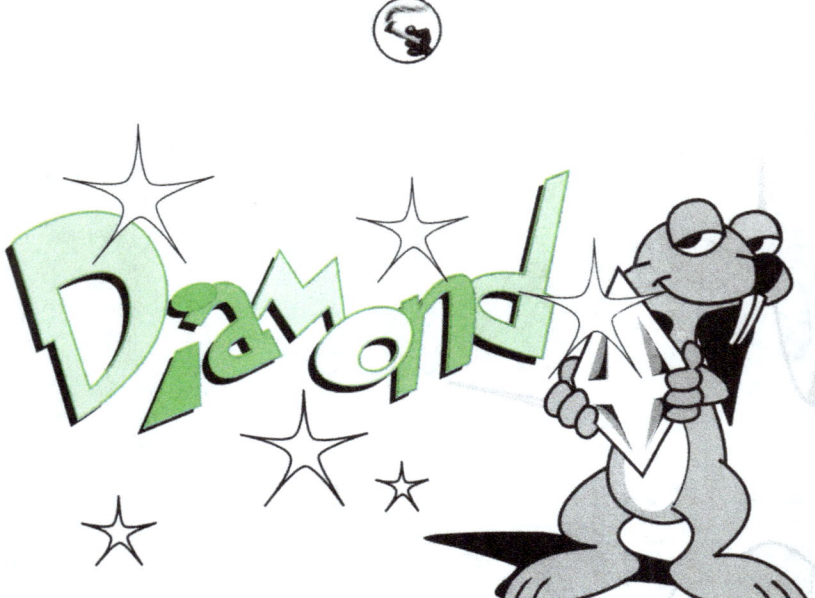

Once mastered, the joining technique opens up a realm of possibilities for weird and fantastic creations. The Diamond is a good place to start and when made with care smokes surprisingly well.

1. Roll a straight, fat joint with a sturdy roach and carefully cut it in half using a pair of scissors or a knife.

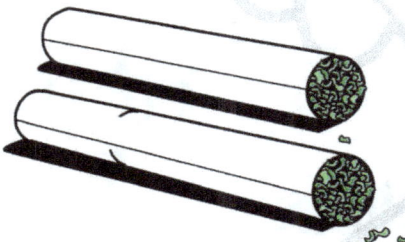

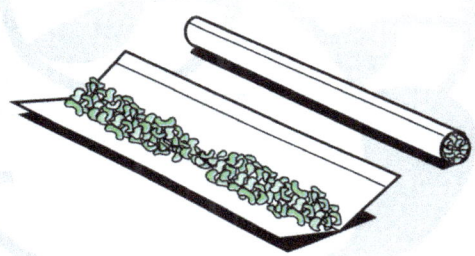

Roll two identical joints, without roaches and slightly thinner than the first. Put slightly less mix in their centers so that you will be able to bend them later on. Consistency is important here, the joints must burn at exactly the same rate.

Carefully trim away any excess paper from all four joints, leaving the mix flush with the paper.

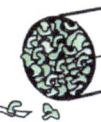

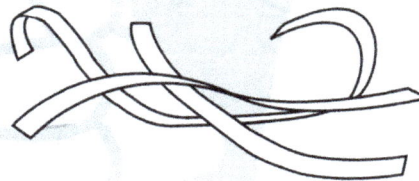

Cut the gummed strips from ten spare papers (the wide strips from large papers are best) and put to one side.

Now for the tricky bit. Join the two identical joints to the segment of the first joint containing the roach. Use some of the gummed strips to bandage the joins as shown. It is best to do this on a flat surface. Keep bandaging until you are confident everything is airtight and secure.

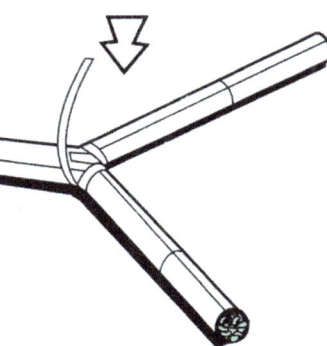

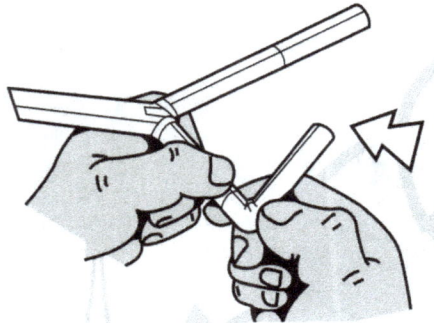

6 Very gently, bend the two joints at their centers until they meet to form a diamond shape.

7 Finally, bandage the remaining joint to the end of the diamond, using the gummed strips as before.

Pat yourself on the back, you're officially a diamond guy!

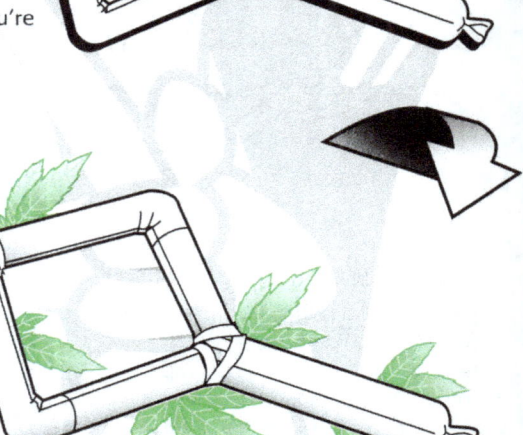

Tulip

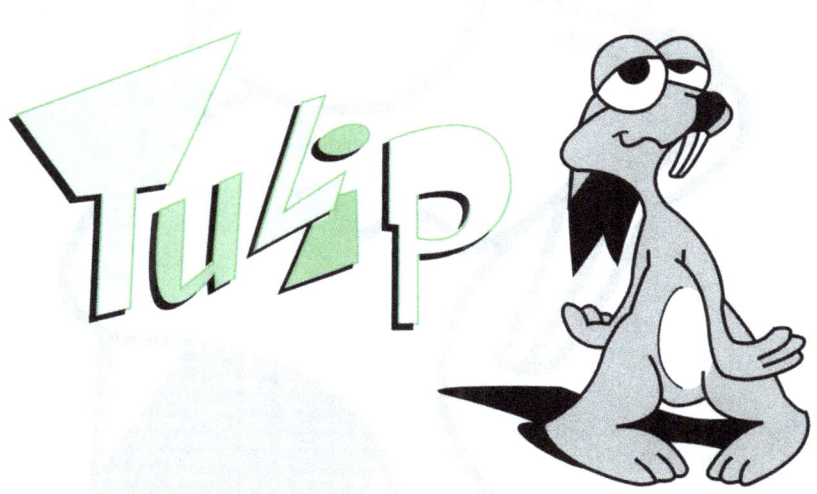

An Amsterdam specialty, the Tulip is often found (usually half-smoked) in the hands of unconscious tourists. A good Tulip is deceptively smooth to smoke and easier to roll than it looks.

1. Make a roach (about the length and diameter of a pencil) and seal it with a couple of large papers.

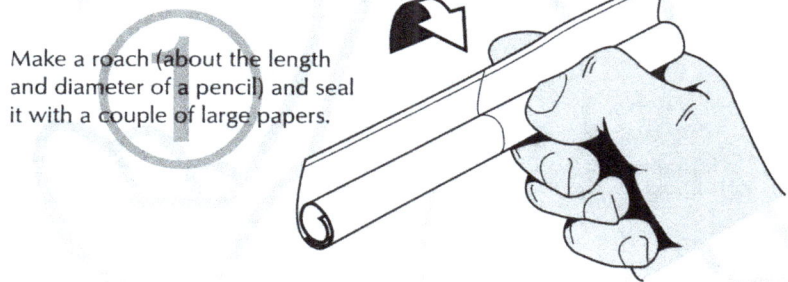

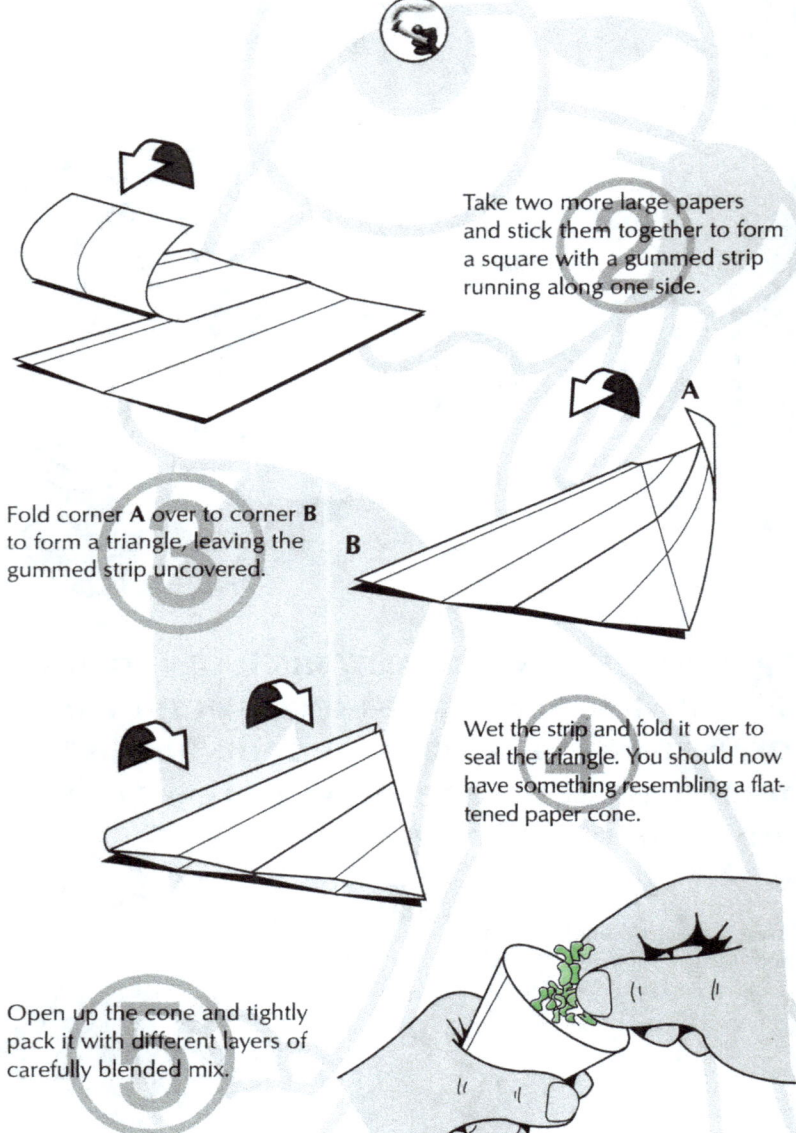

Take two more large papers and stick them together to form a square with a gummed strip running along one side.

Fold corner **A** over to corner **B** to form a triangle, leaving the gummed strip uncovered.

Wet the strip and fold it over to seal the triangle. You should now have something resembling a flattened paper cone.

Open up the cone and tightly pack it with different layers of carefully blended mix.

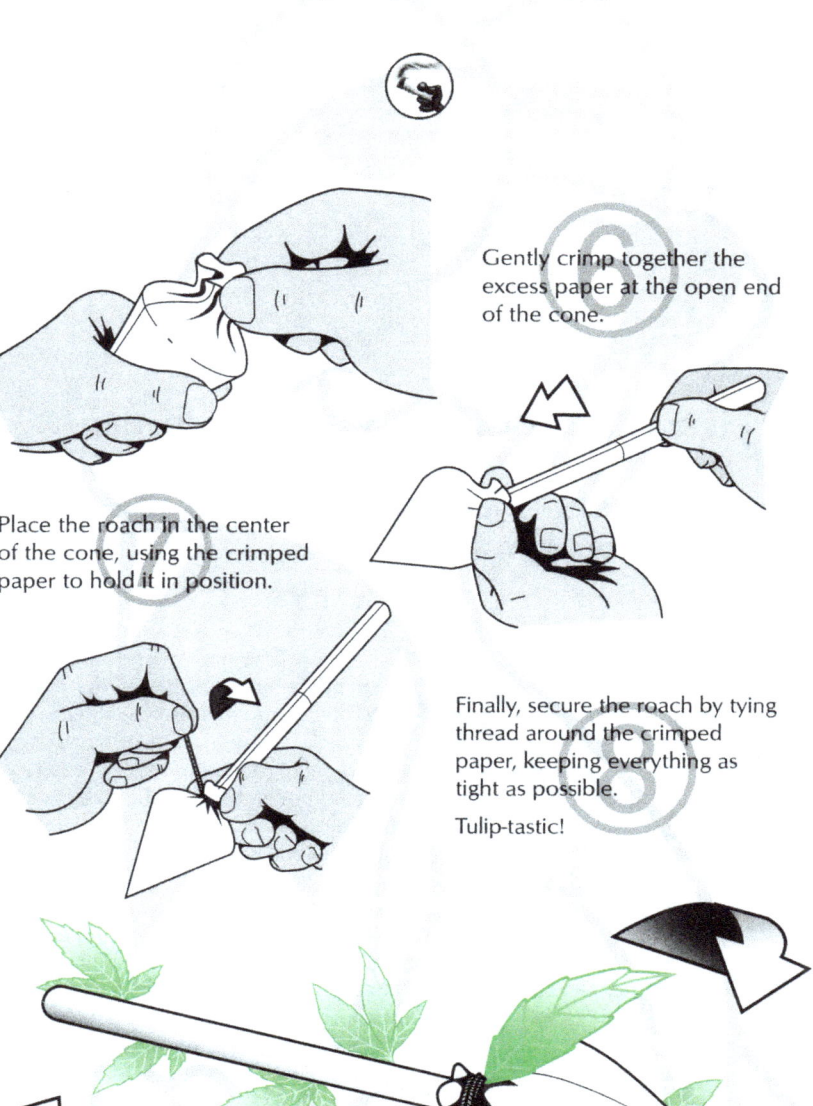

Gently crimp together the excess paper at the open end of the cone.

Place the roach in the center of the cone, using the crimped paper to hold it in position.

Finally, secure the roach by tying thread around the crimped paper, keeping everything as tight as possible.

Tulip-tastic!

PAPER

PAPERS COME IN ALL SHAPES, SIZES, COLORS AND DESIGNS. NOVELTIES ASIDE, THE BEST PAPERS ARE THE ONES WHICH STICK WHERE AND WHEN YOU WANT THEM TO.

There's nothing worse than spending half an hour on your masterpiece only to have it fall apart at the crucial moment. Rice or wheat straw papers are recommended—the thinner and finer the better. Most of the designs in this book are based on rollers using the standard "cigarette-sized" paper but will work equally well with the "king-sized" variety—you'll get bigger joints too.

Paper never got anyone high, so the aim is always to use as little as possible. Try tearing your papers down to size—the smaller the better. Some judicious trimming can also make the joint easier to roll.

The wider, squarer types of paper give you more scope for creating tailor-made papers of different shapes.

If things start to go pear-shaped, the humble paper can save the day. Gummed strips torn from spare papers make excellent bandages for tears, leaks, gaps and other emergencies. The strips are also ideal for creating joins between spliffs or roaches—check out the joint pages for some ideas.

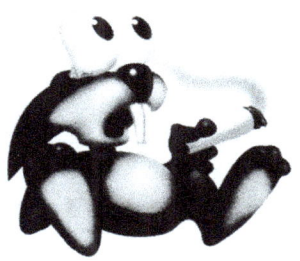

Nose Cone

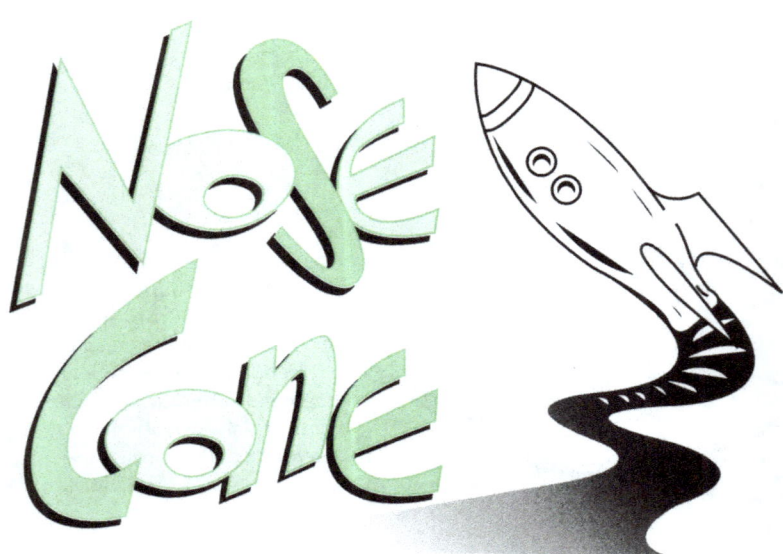

The bigger, badder, bastard brother of the Tulip (try saying that after you've smoked one). It takes some effort to roll, but a good Nose Cone is a king-size chunk of truly cosmic proportions. Lightweights need not apply.

1. Stick two king-size papers together to form a square with a gummed strip running along one side.

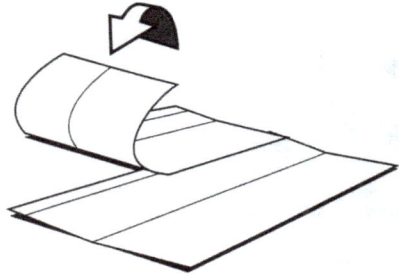

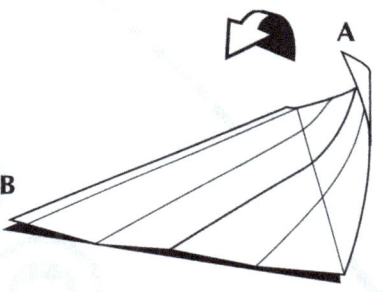

Fold corner **A** over to corner **B** to form a triangle with the gummed strip exposed.

Wet the strip, then fold it over to seal the triangle. You should now have something resembling a flat, paper cone.

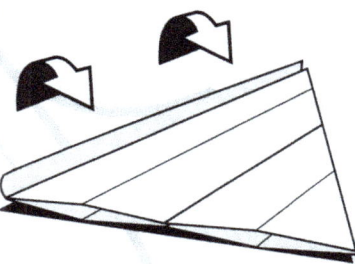

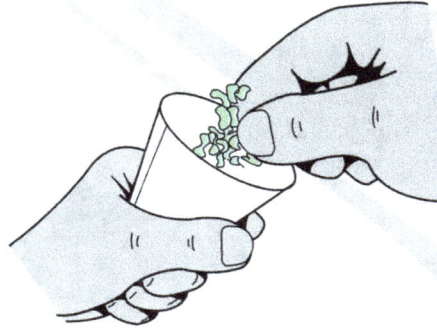

Open up the cone and tightly pack it with layers of different mix.

Take two more king-size papers and stick them together at a 45° angle as shown.

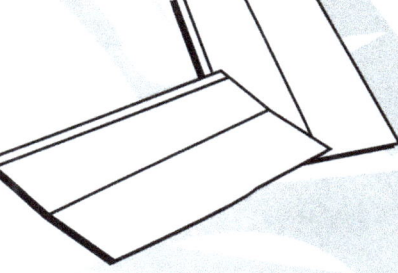

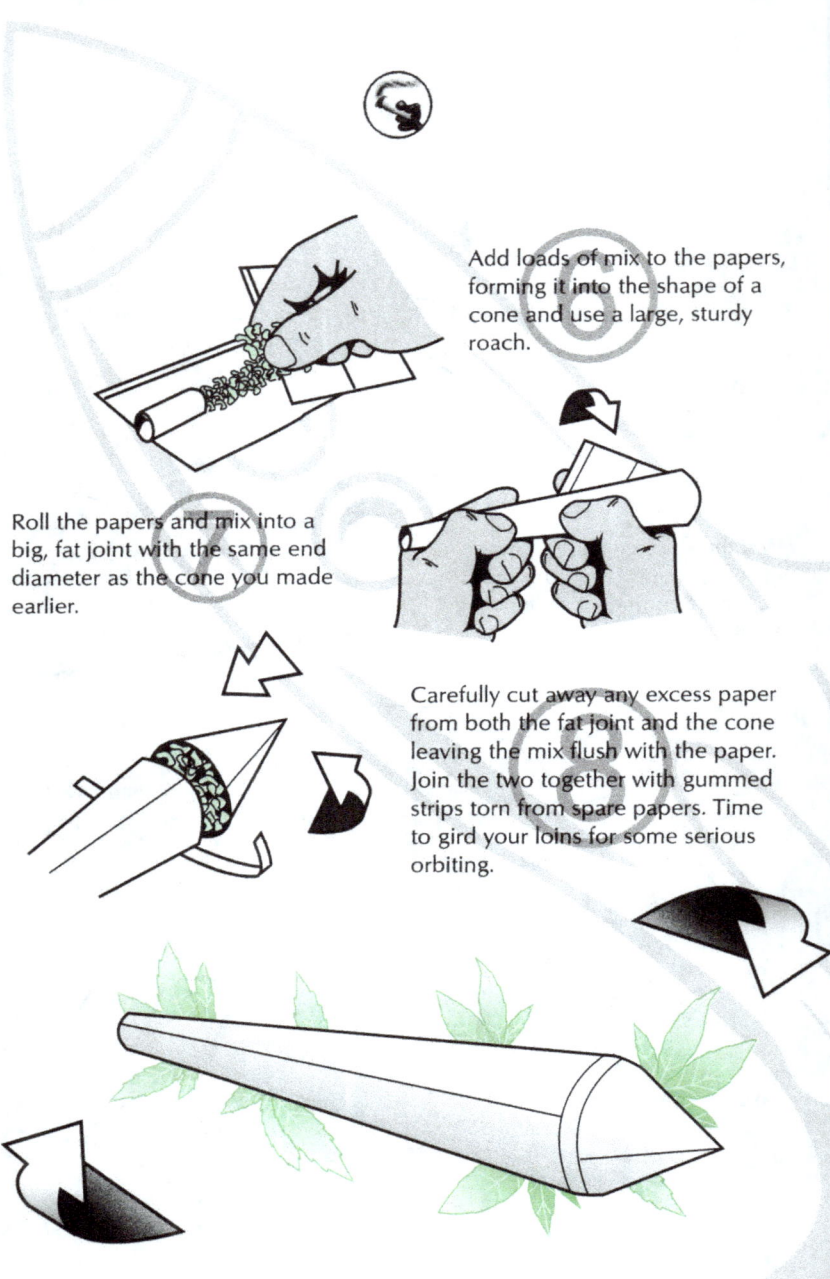

6. Add loads of mix to the papers, forming it into the shape of a cone and use a large, sturdy roach.

7. Roll the papers and mix into a big, fat joint with the same end diameter as the cone you made earlier.

8. Carefully cut away any excess paper from both the fat joint and the cone leaving the mix flush with the paper. Join the two together with gummed strips torn from spare papers. Time to gird your loins for some serious orbiting.

Windmill

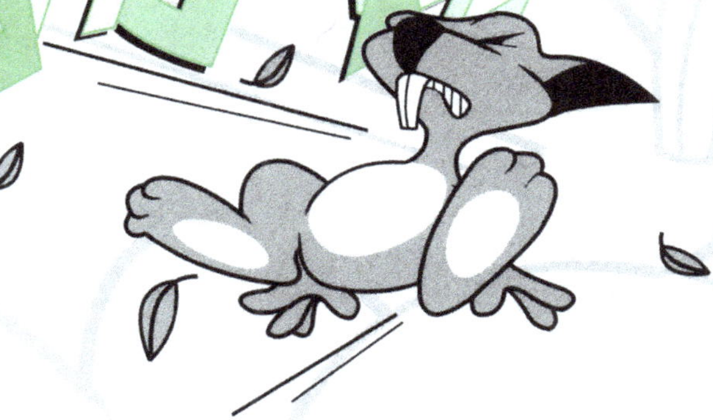

A SMOKE-COOLING CHAMBER AND MULTIPLE JOINT HOLDER, THE WINDMILL IS DESIGNED TO GET YOU SPINNING IN THE BREEZE. ALTHOUGH IT'S TRICKY TO MAKE, THE HOLDER LOOKS GOOD AND CAN BE USED TIME AND TIME AGAIN.

1. Roll a wide cone from a 4 inch by 4 inch piece of cardboard. Secure it with tape then trim the end to form a perfect cone.

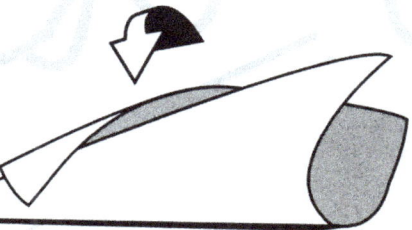

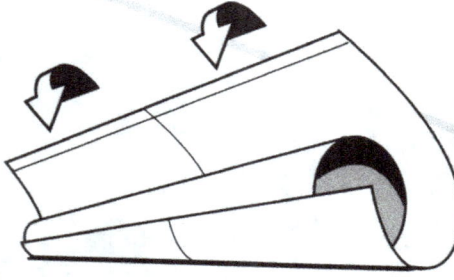

Seal the cone with large papers, leaving 1 1/8 inch of excess paper at the end, as shown.

Carefully make four crosscuts at regular intervals around the end of the cone.

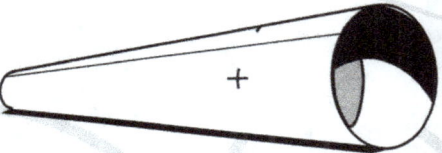

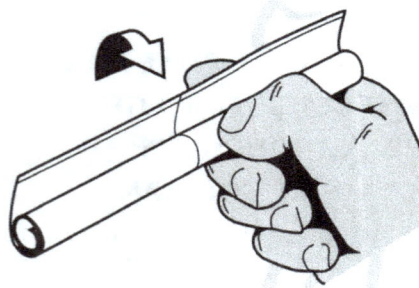

Make a long, narrow roach, about the length of a pencil, and seal it with papers or tape.

Cut the roach in half, then remove a section from the center of each segment.

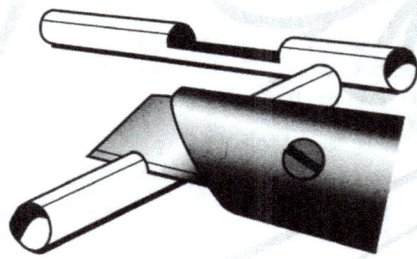

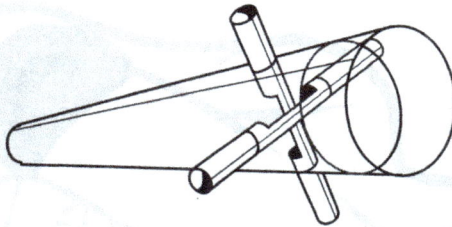

Insert the two segments so that the cut-outs are completely inside the cone and facing its narrow end. Seal any gaps with tape or gummed strips.

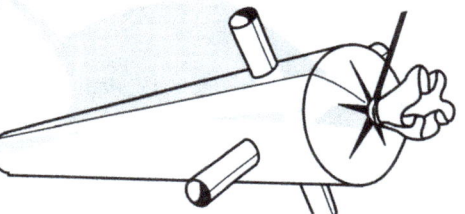

Seal the end of the Windmill with the excess paper, using thread or tape.

To use the Windmill, roll the joints of your choice around the protruding roaches and enjoy a four-way smoke of quixotic proportions.

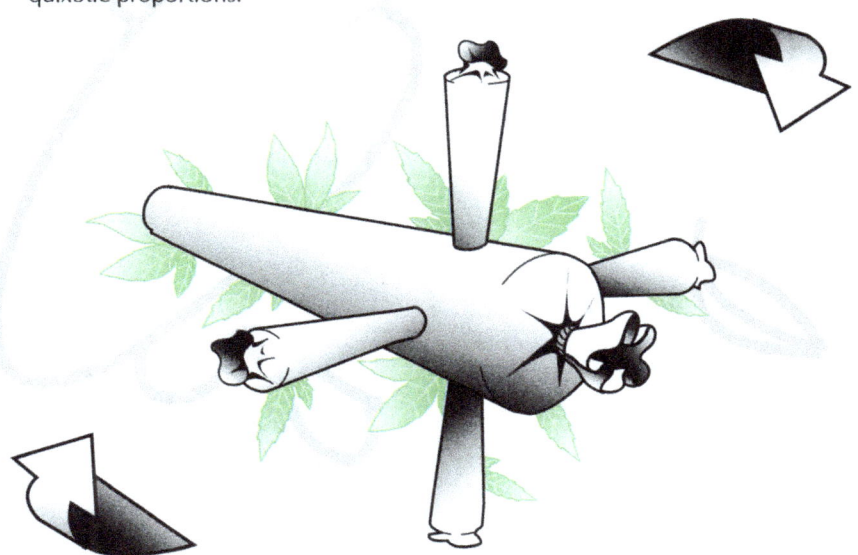

Cannabis Cigar

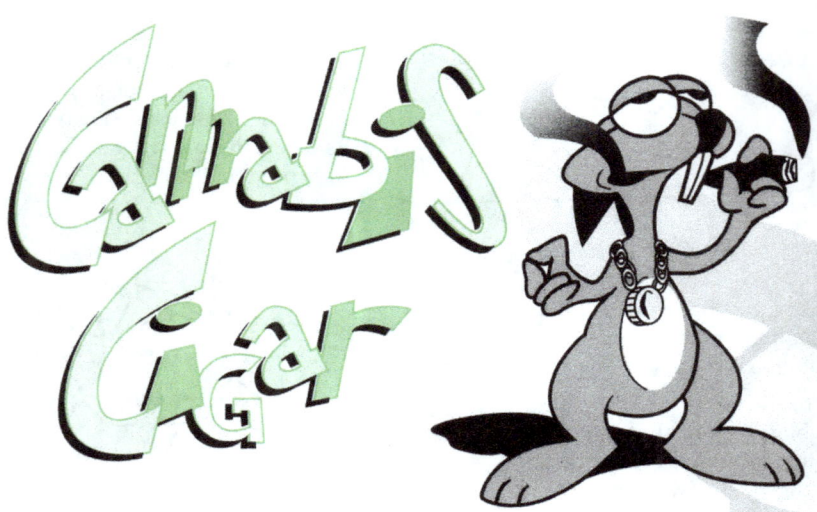

A PURE CANNABIS CIGAR IS PERHAPS THE ULTIMATE JOINT AND A MUST FOR THE RICH, FAMOUS AND WELL-CONNECTED. USING EXOTIC, HARD-TO-FIND INGREDIENTS, THIS CAN BE A HARD ONE TO PULL TOGETHER.

First, find yourself a Thai stick, (cured buds tied around a bamboo sliver) remove any thread and carefully coat it with liquid cannabis resin oil.

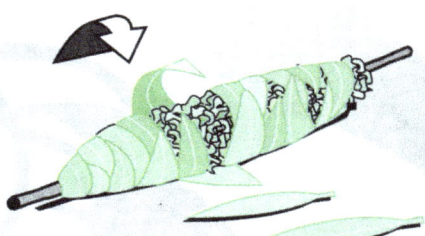

Wrap the coated stick with small, uncured, "top" leaves, remembering to remove any stems.

Secure the leaves with thread and coat with more liquid resin. Leave the cigar to dry in a dark, dry and warm place for a day or so.

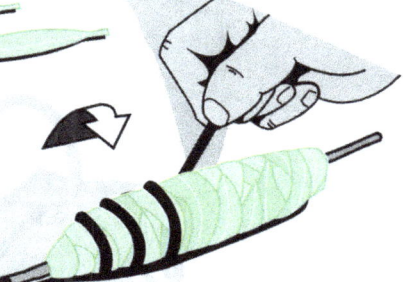

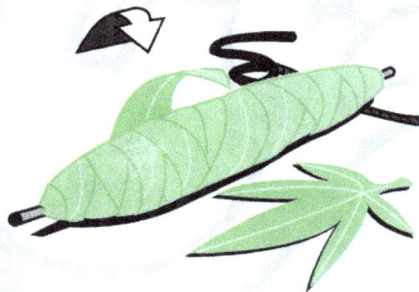

Remove the thread and repeat the entire process. Use progressively larger cannabis leaves until the cigar is suitably fat.

Use large "sun" leaves to seal the cigar, add a final coat of cannabis resin and secure with more thread.

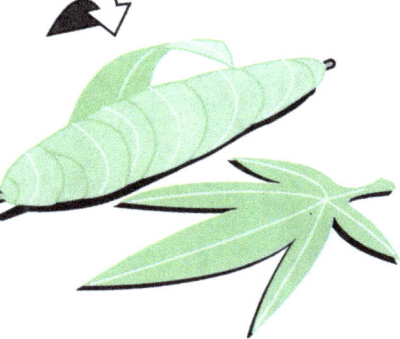

Leave the finished cigar to dry. In two to three weeks it should be ready to smoke.

When drying is complete, remove the thread and carefully pull the bamboo sliver from inside the cigar to create a smoking tube.

Store your cigars in a dry, airtight container—the longer you leave them, the better (and stronger) they will get.

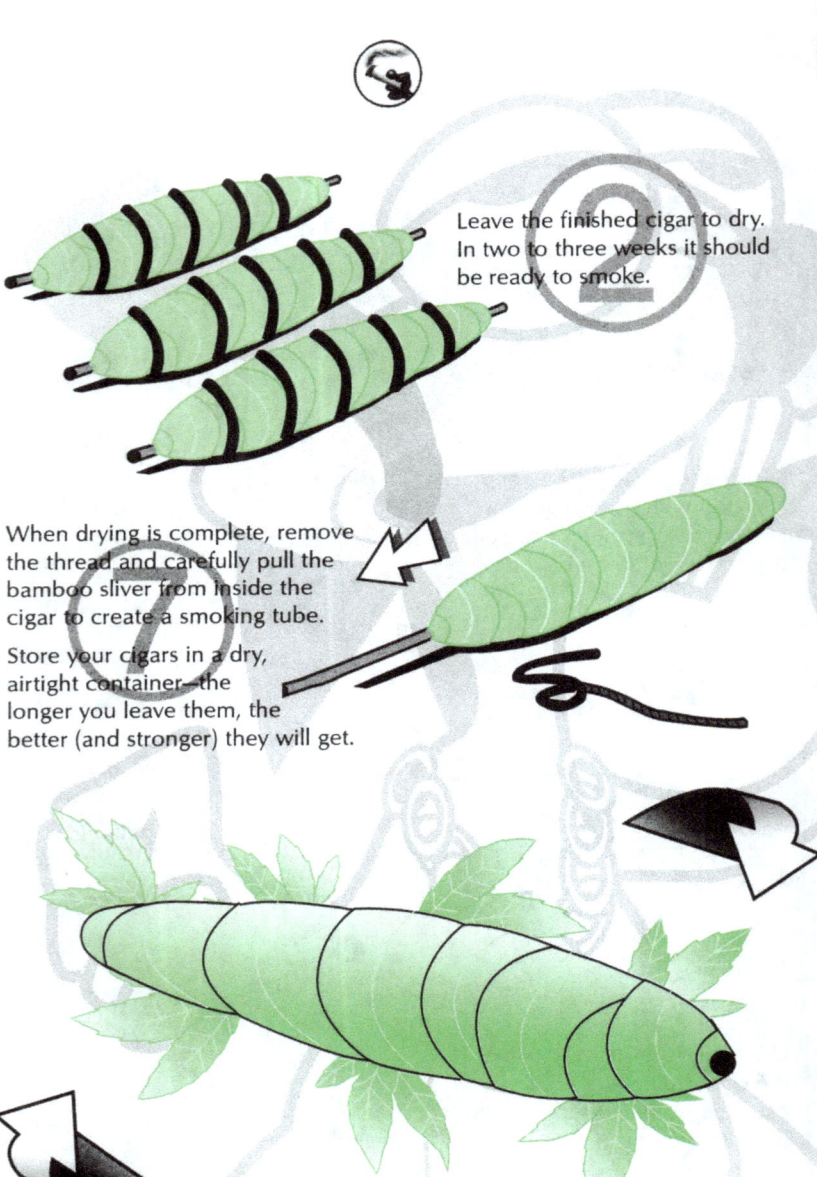

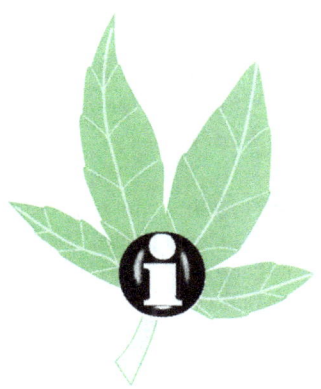

1

WHAT IS IT?
—CANNABIS THE PLANT

Cannabis (or **hemp**) together with hops, is one of the main genera of the Cannabaceae family of plants. There are generally agreed to be three species of cannabis—cannabis *sativa*, cannabis *indica* and cannabis *ruderalis*—although some botanists suggest the latter two are, in fact, sub-species of sativa. Cannabis is a tough, fast growing annual plant that can reach over 20 feet in height and tolerate a wide variety of conditions. The plant has enjoyed a symbiotic relationship with humans throughout history and has been spread and cultivated all over the planet.

WHAT IS IT FOR?

GETTING HIGH

There are records dating back to 2737 BC of cannabis being used for its psychoactive effects in medicine, recreation and religious ceremonies.

Cannabis has an unusually complex chemical make-up. The smoke produced when cannabis is burnt contains over 400 different chemicals, 60 of which are cannabinoids. So far only a few of the cannabinoids have been identified as psychoactive, the main three being tetrahydrocannabinol (**THC**), cannabidiol (**CBD**) and cannabinol (**CBN**). THC is, by far, the most active of these three.

When inhaled, THC travels from the lungs into the bloodstream and then directly on to the brain where it targets brain cell receptors concerned with memory, emotion and coordination of movement. In 1992, a naturally produced neurotransmitter—***anandamide*** (a name derived from *ananda,* the Sanskrit word for bliss)—was found to target the same receptors, mirroring the effects of THC.

SAVING THE PLANET

There is evidence to suggest that the human race has been using cannabis for over 8,000 years. Until the 20th century and the spread of prohibition, cannabis was the most common agricultural crop in the world. The Business Alliance For Commerce In Hemp has so far recorded over 50,000 non-smoking, commercial uses for the plant. In short, it does a lot more than get people high. Environmentalists and forward-thinking industrialists alike point to cannabis as a highly feasible, entirely sustainable and, in many cases, far superior substitute for fossil fuels and woodland in the production of paper, textiles, construction materials, plastics and even petroleum.

② BEING STONED

—SHORT-TERM EFFECTS OF CANNABIS USE

Cannabis is unusual in that it produces effects similar to those of many different psychoactive substances. The drug does not easily slot into any of the normal psychoactive groups (depressants, stimulants, hallucinogens) and displays characteristics distinctive to all three. For instance, a group of people using cannabis may swing from introspective states of dreamy detachment to high-energy conversation and collective euphoria.

The short-term effects of cannabis use are largely dependent on the quality of the substance and the individual's mood, personality and previous experience. Studies show a marked difference in effects between "first-timers" and "veteran" smokers. It seems that with repeated use a user learns to anticipate, recognize and enjoy the effects while an inexperienced smoker may simply feel confused and dizzy. Environment and company also influence the experience. For instance, subject X smoking a joint in a room crowded with strangers might experience paranoia and fear while subject X smoking an identical joint in a room with a few close friends might feel particularly relaxed and at ease.

Ⓐ Subjective Effects

Pleasant

Some of the more common subjectively positive experiences include the following (often in this order):

① Euphoria and/or a feeling of general well-being;

② Uncontrollable hilarity (or "the giggles");

③ Increased sociability and talkativeness ;

④ Enhanced perception of colors, music, film, art, nature, wallpaper, etc.;

⑤ Increased mental energy, lateral thinking and creativity;

⑥ Major changes in consciousness (man);

⑦ Distortion of time and space;

⑧ A ravenous appetite (or "the munchies").

Unpleasant

Negative subjective effects, more common among new users may include the following:

① Forgetting what one was saying, thinking or doing, often in the middle of saying th . . . Umm, sorry, what was I saying?

② Paranoia—often related to the fact that the user is aware they are breaking the law;

③ Anxiety and confusion;

④ Fatigue and drowsiness;

⑤ Ordering pizza at 4 a.m.;

⑥ Losing your keys.

Driving ability is adversely effected by cannabis use although recent research suggests impairment is much less serious than that caused by alcohol use.

3

POST-STONED
—LONG-TERM EFFECTS OF CANNABIS USE

For such a widely researched drug, a lot of controversy and confusion still surround cannabis and its long-term effects on users' health. Studies have been repeatedly debunked as politically-motivated scare mongering or just plain bad science. Many of the flaws in the investigations revolve around a failure to relate to the actual use of cannabis in "real life."

In truth there is little sound evidence to suggest that long-term cannabis use singularly causes significant physical or mental health problems. In fact, a recent examination of the available material in The Lancet (11th November 1995) concluded: "The smoking of cannabis even long-term is not harmful to health," others might disagree. So let's take a look at some of the claims relating to long-term effects on the human mind and body.

Ⓐ THE MIND

There's no doubt that cannabis has a profound effect on the mind during intoxication but arguments of enduring effects are hotly contested. A complicating factor is that, as cannabinoids stay in the body for up to fifty days, there is a danger of residual effects being confused with permanent damage or change.

Motivation

The occasional forgetfulness and lethargy (so-called ***amotivational syndrome***) that affects some heavy cannabis users seems to be dependent on continued use and/or the normal personality of the individual. Much of the thinking surrounding amotivational syndrome is rooted in the establishment view that cannabis is a primary cause for social unrest and deviancy. There is no evidence at all of an enduring effect after use is discontinued and many heavy users lead complex and busy lives without apparent difficulty.

Dependence and Tolerance

Cannabis is often called a non-addictive drug. However, as with most drugs (including tea and coffee), an element of social or psychological dependence is possible for some users or groups of users. Cannabis "habits" tend to be based around the simple desire to repeat a pleasurable experience rather than real compulsion. Problematic addiction that seriously interferes with a user's normal life seems to be very rare indeed. It is unclear whether tolerance to the effects of cannabis does develop with continued use or whether it is more of a case of users adjusting to, and learning to cope with, their "altered" states.

Mental Illness

Claims that cannabis can cause or trigger serious mental illness have been common ever since the Reefer Madness propaganda of the 1930s. In fact there is no evidence to show that lasting mental disorder can be directly caused by cannabis. Whether the drug may trigger a latent illness, or worsen (or even improve) an existing one is open to debate as there are a myriad of everyday elements in a person's life (work, relationships, etc.) which also have that capability.

The Body

Respiratory Disease

The smoke from a pure cannabis joint delivers three times more tar than your standard filter-tip cigarette, more than five times more carbon monoxide, and hits the throat and lungs at a higher temperature. This has lead some experts to declare that, blow-for-blow, cannabis smoke is more likely to cause respiratory disease and cancer of the lungs, throat and mouth than tobacco smoke. Other experts point to increasing evidence that cancer is caused primarily by the radiation present in tobacco tar and that the carcinogenic nature of cannabis is wildly overstated. In any case, comparison with tobacco should be tempered by the fact that a twenty-a-day habit of unshared pure joints is relatively rare.

There is no conclusive evidence that moderate cannabis use leads to significant damage to the respiratory system. However, a tobacco/cannabis joint carries the same risks as an unfiltered cigarette.

Central Nervous System

Both reputable and highly disreputable sources have put forward the claim that cannabis causes brain cell death. Such claims are highly controversial and no permanent effects have ever been demonstrated in humans. Whatever the truth of the matter, there is no evidence to suggest that the "possible" damage would cause any significant change in behavior or mental performance.

Reproduction

Bizarre claims that cannabis reduces libido, causes men to grow breasts, and disrupts menstruation in women have been circulated since the '60s. You won't be surprised to hear that, yet again, there is no scientific basis for these claims.

Male cannabis users do produce a higher proportion of two-tailed spermatozoa which tend to be too confused to make it to the ovum. However, coffee drinkers also experience this phenomenon and smokers will be relieved to know that there are usually millions of the single-tailed variety ready to step in and that, in any case, the genetic coding of the sperm is not effected.

IMMUNOLOGY

There is some evidence, both real and anecdotal, to suggest that cannabis may have an effect on a user's immunity from disease, although there is nothing to show that this is any more significant than that suffered with the similar effects of moderate alcohol or caffeine use. Much of the evidence may originate from contagious diseases (especially the common cold) hitching a ride on joints passed between friends.

4

CAUGHT STONED
—LEGAL AND SOCIAL IMPLICATIONS OF CANNABIS USE

Estimates put the number of regular cannabis users in the United States at between ten and fifteen million, with more than one in three young adults thought to have tried the drug at least once. Smoking cannabis is now common outside of its traditional sub-cultural environment and is seen as an increasingly acceptable activity throughout all of society. Whether this trend will continue is another matter and, for the time being, cannabis is still very much a controlled substance with users running the risk of prosecution and prejudice from the establishment and employment markets.

Ⓐ CANNABIS AND THE LAW

U.S. drug law is infamous for being tough on offenders. You need only consider the **War on Drugs** of the '80s and mandatory minimum sentencing of the '90s to know that drug users and growers must tread carefully to avoid detection by authorities.

FEDERAL AND STATE LAW

Cannabis laws can vary from state to state and sometimes conflict with federal laws. For example, California now allows the use of cannabis for medical purposes, but federal agents continue to seize paraphernalia used to grow or distribute cannabis, even when it is grown for use as a medicine.

Confused? You soon will be. When it comes to breaking the law with cannabis, there is plenty of scope.

Of course, the best advice is not to get caught, but just in case, get to know the consequences of cannabis use in your state. Your local NORML chapter is a good source of information.

USE/UNDER THE INFLUENCE

Driving under the influence can lead to loss of your license and jail time. Being involved in an accident while under the influence makes you entirely responsible, even if the other driver was at fault.

POSSESSION

Possession can include possession of cannabis, or possession of paraphernalia for use in the sale or trafficking of cannabis. The penalties of an amount of cannabis for personal use vary from state to state. If you are suspected of trafficking or selling cannabis, the authorities have the right to seize any or all property suspected to be used for trafficking or selling the drug, and any assets purchased with profits from traffic or sales. This includes everything from weighing instruments, to your car, house, or your bank account. Be very careful not to incriminate yourself as a dealer.

SUPPLY

Supply, a.k.a. distribution, a.k.a. sale, a.k.a. trafficking, can range from passing a joint to importing tons of hashish. The guidelines on sentencing for trafficking are based on a sliding scale relating to the offense and amounts involved. Custodial sentences are common at the mid- to high-end of this scale.

As with possession, there is a group of offenses which can be listed as trafficking: ***possession with intent to supply***—where there is evidence that the amounts found are not purely for personal use; ***offering to supply***; ***conspiracy to supply***; etc.

CULTIVATION

Needless to say, growing cannabis in the United States is illegal without government permission, or—in California—without the recommendation or prescription of a physician (and then, only for personal use). The real problem for growers arises when the amounts are significant in the eyes of the law and attract additional charges of intent to supply or trafficking. As with possession and supply, strong mitigating factors can come into effect if the substances found are deemed to be for personal or medical use, but again, be aware of the limits imposed in your state to avoid incurring additional charges which can result in long prison terms or seizure of property.

B OTHER IMPLICATIONS

Conviction for a cannabis-related offense can leave you with more than just jail time. Due to a number of laws, institutional practices and societal attitudes toward drug users in general, the consequences of a cannabis conviction can be far-reaching and may include the following:

1) Being excluded from particular careers—employers don't look kindly on drug convictions;

2) Public humiliation—local newspapers (especially those of the small town variety) love a drug story;

3) Being banned from driving if convicted of driving while under the influence;

4) Refusal of bank loans or credit if convicted of supplying or intent to supply;

5) Refusal of immigration requests and even temporary visas for work or holidays by some countries;

6) Possible difficulties with fostering or adoption proceedings and, in some extreme cases, the removal of children into care.

Self-Protection

The best advice for avoiding prosecution is, of course, not to commit an offense. Social acceptance of cannabis use in youth culture and subcultures can lead to an over-casual attitude toward the drug. It is worth bearing in mind that over 85% of cannabis-related convictions are for simple possession of cannabis—not for the sale or manufacture of the drug. The second-best advice for avoiding prosecution is to be very, very careful. Being charged with offenses more serious than justified is sadly a common occurrence. Weighing instruments, a divided stash or large amounts of the drug can mean a charge of intent to supply rather than one of simple possession. Helping out your friends, especially on a regular basis, can be a risky business.

Suspicion of cannabis possession is frequently given as a reason for police to stop and search, and suspicion of supplying cannabis allows authorization for search warrants and seizure of property.

If you are arrested by the police, the best advice is to know your rights. Do not admit to an offense or otherwise incriminate yourself before obtaining the advice of a lawyer, to which you are entitled by law.

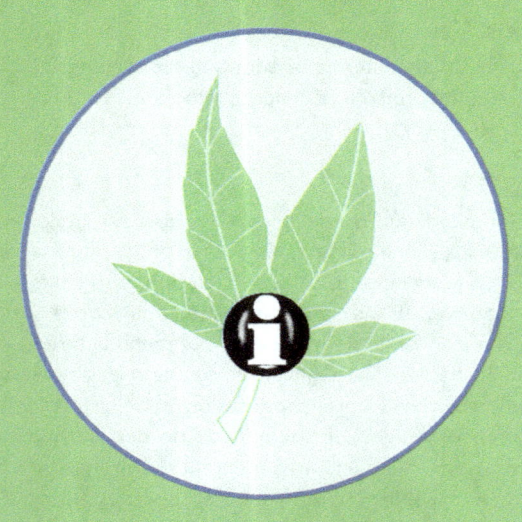